To Stu...
Always be
Extreme!

CW00540828

Rory GBR
705

# A Rebel and a Runner

Rory Coleman

Matador
9 Priory Business Park,
Wistow Road, Kibworth Beauchamp,
Leicestershire. LE8 0RX
Tel: 0116 279 2299
Email: books@troubador.co.uk
Web: www.troubador.co.uk/matador
Twitter: @matadorbooks

ISBN 978 1788036 757

British Library Cataloguing in Publication Data.
A catalogue record for this book is available from the British Library.

Printed and bound by CPI Group (UK) Ltd, Croydon, CR0 4YY
Typeset in 11pt Minion Pro by Troubador Publishing Ltd, Leicester, UK

Matador is an imprint of Troubador Publishing Ltd

MIX
Paper from
responsible sources
FSC
www.fsc.org     FSC® C013604

*To my wife Jenny and children Hannah, George, Sam, Pearl, Jack and Charlie.*

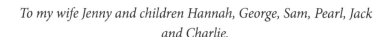

## ACKNOWLEDGEMENTS

My heart-felt thanks go to my good friend Ben Wilson who told me I must write a book and helped me to record the whole 'A Rebel and a Runner' story during countless hours of conversations together. Thanks also to Samantha Wood from Transcription Services Ltd who was tasked with typing them out, minus the swearing and laughter, before my editing and rewriting process. Finally to my wife, Jenny, who went through the whole book with a fine toothcomb perfecting my grammar, punctuation and spelling.

# Foreword

*So Why the Book?*

I want to share my life-story from being a real 'Rebel' to becoming a World Record Breaking 'Runner'. As you will discover, the journey isn't a nice straight line - it has many twists and turns along the way. The process of writing it all down has proved a journey in itself where I've been able to relive the highs and lows associated with ultra-marathon running and with life itself. The book culminates in a triumphant finish at Trafalgar Square on my 23rd ultra-marathon in 23 days as part of the government's Stoptober campaign as Britain's Most Extreme Runner. I hope you enjoy reading about my exploits - I've worked out that you don't need to be a Rebel to make your mark in life... you just need to be a Runner.

*So Why the Music?*

Music plays an important part in my life and has partnered me through the good and the not so good times. Songs trigger certain memories and have accompanied me on my journeys the world over as well as during the hours and hours of training. I'm lucky that I've grown up in such an era of change in popular music. I'm old enough to remember the heights of Prog Rock and have lived through Punk, the New Romantics, Brit Pop and Drum and Bass. I love a complete spectrum of musical style. Throughout the book you'll find my 'Top 12 Desert Island can't-do-without Discs' and the reasons why they are so important to me. Narrowing it down to just twelve has proved to be a marathon in itself and I can only apologise, to myself, if I've forgotten ones I should have chosen. Here they are…

*New World Man - Rush 1982*

This is a real anthem for me - I was lucky enough to see Rush in 1981 on their 'Exit…Stage Left World Tour' at New Bingley Hall in Stafford. I couldn't hear for days after that gig as they were unbelievably loud. I've literally run thousands of miles listening to Rush and could have chosen a Rush song for every chapter of the book. Although this is a relatively short song for the Canadian Rock Trio at 3:39 minutes, it's a great example of the sheer volume of their music. It feels like the lyrics, written by drummer Neil Peart, were written with me in mind and I feel like a New World Man every single time I hear it.

*Sheep - Pink Floyd 1977*

I must have played this song a thousand times and it's my all-time 'Floyd Favourite'. Roger Waters' vitriolic lyrics describe the worst trait ever - being a 'Sheep', being someone that follows someone else's path and goes with the flock instead of being prepared to 'Stick Out' from the crowd. I've looked out over Jordan, just like the lyrics say, and the Psalm 23 parody is just priceless. The creativity of each phase of the 10 minute track amazes me each and every time I listen to it. There's a great live version on the 'Wish You Were Here' remastered album from 1974 ('Raving & Drooling') which is well worth a listen. The drive and ambition I've gained from this track over the years has been immense and I don't think songs gets much better than this one. Remember, 'Get out of the road, if you want to grow old.' It's a great adage.

*Secret World (Live) - Peter Gabriel 1992*

As an all-time hero of mine, this track encompasses everything that is simply brilliant about Gabriel's music. I somehow missed the original on his 'US' album and the subsequent tour, much to my dismay. On first hearing, this was an instant hit for me and the 'Live' version has a slight edge over the studio recording in my opinion. Having lived in many different 'Secret Worlds' during my lifetime the 'Breaking it Up, Shaking it Up' reflects the many regenerations I've been through. I love the gentle build and crescendo of the track and Gabriel's vocals in both low and high range are really powerful.

*Fly on a Windshield - Genesis 1974*

This is 'Real Genesis' (Banks, Collins, Gabriel, Hackett & Rutherford) at their peak in my opinion. I love the anticipation as the mood of this multi-layered music builds in true prog rock fashion right up until the drums and lead guitar kick in half-way through. The track segways into Broadway Melody of 1974 which I could have also chosen but I like the way I'm always left wanting more of everything after listening to this song and often play it over and over again on runs. The lyrics mirror my feelings about writing this book and how I feel now that I'm at the start of a whole new journey.

*Uninvited - Freemasons (featuring Bailey Tzuke) 2007*

The Freemasons' Production Team of Russell Small and James Wiltshire injected the X-Factor into this brilliant rework of Alanis Morissette's rather dark original, making it a stand out track for me. This track was played on a loop at Fitness First in Derby, where I worked out of for three years, so it must have been drilled deep down into my sub-consciousness. For me, there's a fantastic feel-good factor that accompanies this song because I loved that time in my life where I was learning and starting over professionally.

## Highway to Hell - AC/DC 1979

If ever a race had a song that described it, the Aussie Rockers did just the job for the Marathon des Sables. I've lost count of the amount of times I've sung along to this classic in the start pen of the MdS while Race Director, Patrick Bauer, sang along in Franglais, 'Ighway to 'Ell.' I laugh every time it's played as it's so heartily sung along to before people are literally taken to hell and back. It was the last album featuring lead singer Bon Scott who died in 1980 from consuming too much alcohol. This seems quite poignant. It's possibly the best of all of the AC/DC anthems helped along by a huge dose of magic by Music Producer Robert 'Mutt' Lange.

## Welcome to the Machine - Pink Floyd 1975

This is total 'Headphone Heaven' for me. The stereo effects are as alive today as they were some forty years ago. Hearing it now as it was recorded is simply amazing. The days of my Pioneer Cassette Deck, no matter how great I thought it was at the time, couldn't cope with the hiss even though it was Dolby C. I've always thought that life feels like being part of a machine and apart from being asked where you've been, you're asked what did you dream? That's a really important line for me as without a dream, well there's no vision and without a vision there's no direction, something that I can't live without.

## Inside Out (Live) - Phil Collins 1985

Phil Collins is at his best with this mid-eighties classic. Only ten years prior to this he was drumming on the classic 'The Lamb Lies Down on Broadway' double Genesis Album. Here he's Producer, Song-writer, Pianist and Drummer surrounded by a great live act including Chester Thompson on Drums and

Daryl Stuermer on lead guitar. The lead solo is one of my favourites of all time because it's so well-crafted. Funnily enough, Peter Gabriel is on backing vocals. Talk about full circle!

*Laid so Low - Tear for Fears 1992*

If you ever decide to run from London to Lisbon, you'll need this. It's Roland Orzabal at his best. Having chewed that bone far too low, I shed many tears listening to this over and over again on my 1,275-mile journey. Lyrically perfect in so many ways, it also showcases Orzabal's all-round musicianship including a great guitar solo. It's one of those tracks that unfortunately fades out and when the fade starts I hit replay.

*Pendulum - 9000 Miles 2008*

I'll admit I'm a late convert to the Aussie Drum and Bass Duo but I bought all three studio albums in quick succession. It's loud, fast, melodic and really, really clever stuff. Robert Swire-Thompson is such a great Lead-Singer/Producer and there are some amazing live Glastonbury performances on YouTube that are well worth a look. The bass rattles my walls at home and really makes the sub come to life. It's music that makes you feel as though you've known it all your life yet it's still completely fresh. It's great running music and you will soon get the feel of the 'Pendulum' kicking in when each track gets going.

*Shaking the Tree (Live) - Peter Gabriel 1989*

A second track for Sir Peter of Gabriel and why not? This live version is very different to the original with Youssou N'Dour and benefits greatly from the additional vocals of Paula Cole. The band includes Tony Levin on bass and David Rhodes on lead guitar as well as Manu Katche on drums. They play so tightly together that the whole 'Secret World' album is a total triumph and is in fact my favourite live album. There's a great video of the album too that's well worth a view.

*And I will Kiss - Underworld 2012*

During the opening ceremony of the 2012 London Olympics there was a moment that I'll never forget. To be honest, I had pretty low expectations and was looking at Danny Boyle's £9m creation in mild disbelief at the beginning of the show. Then, over the course of a few minutes, it transformed into a jaw-dropping spectacle that made every hair on my body stand on end. The 17:15 minute track was written by Underworld's Rick Smith and features 1,200 musicians including Dame Evelyn Glennie on percussion and The Pandemonium Drummers. The ceremony's grand finale featured Sir Kenneth Branagh as Sir Isambard Kingdom Brunel and there was a breathtaking moment where all five blazing rings were hoisted into place to finally pour molten sparks to the ground. The title makes reference to a speech given by Caliban in Act 2, Scene 2 of The Tempest by William Shakespeare which seems so apt given my Stratford-upon-Avon connection. I have run some of my fastest times listening to this track as it's so inspiring.

# INTRODUCTION

## NEW WORLD MAN - RUSH 1982

*This is a real anthem for me - I was lucky enough to see Rush in 1981 on their 'Exit...Stage Left World Tour' at New Bingley Hall in Stafford. I couldn't hear for days after that gig as they were unbelievably loud. I've literally run thousands of miles listening to Rush and could have chosen a Rush song for every chapter of the book. Although this is a relatively short song for the Canadian Rock Trio at 3:39 minutes, it's a great example of the sheer volume of their music. It feels like the lyrics, written by drummer Neil Peart, were written with me in mind and I feel like a New World Man every single time I hear it.*

If there is one race that, for me, epitomises the agony and the ecstasy of long-distance running, it's the Marathon des Sables ('MdS')... more specifically the 2006 edition. The MdS is billed as 'The World's Toughest Footrace' - it's a six-day ultra-marathon that traverses mountains and crosses endless miles of sand dunes in the Sahara Desert, Morocco. The heat is excruciating. Everyone in the race that year, including me, was suffering big time - physically, mentally and spiritually.

But even amidst the hell and the heat, I loved it.

As Britain's Most Extreme Runner, this newfound passion for pushing myself to the limit consolidated my mind-set that this was what I was born to do. This, I realised, was my version of therapy - amidst the horror I was cleansing my soul.

I'd first run the race in 1999. Seven years later, following a few personal ups and downs, I'd completed lots of other extreme challenges and races and all I was hoping to do, looking in my rear view mirrors with my rose-tinted spectacles, was to go and drink in some more of that old 'Marathon des Sables Magic'.

So I rocked up at the start line thinking it was going to be just another day at the office. Funnily enough it was the 'Jack Osbourne year' - the year that Ozzy Osbourne's son had entered the race to be filmed as part of a series of programmes he featured in called 'Adrenaline Junkie'. For some reason this made me feel even more at ease - I figured if he could do it then I'd sail through. I met him on the first day - he was great, a really nice lad. He's about the same age as one of my sons and was only 20 at the time. We had a bit in common because of his alcohol addiction, so we spoke about that. In fact I felt so confident that I even found myself saying, 'If you want to complete the race, Jack, just stay with me and I'll get you to the finish.'

By Day Two, the MdS had broken Jack and I was in pieces.

What on earth had happened to the MdS? The desert had been really arid back in 1999 - the first year I'd taken part - and the heat and humidity hadn't really affected me. For some reason though, in 2006 it felt a lot hotter and the humidity had really peaked. Nobody had a clue what was going on and no-one really knew how much salt we needed to take in our water to fend off that crazy heat.

What had started off as just another MdS had become a real-life Vietnam War. I'm not kidding, it was total carnage and the race doctors were stretched to their limits. Their only option was to place the really sick runners into enforced comas. Competitors were hyper-thermic as they'd simply cooked out there in the sand. It was well over 50°C and the humidity was well over 25%. It was so hot and humid it wasn't only dangerous, it became life-threatening.

The humidity in 1999 had been a very dry 5-6%, so although it was extremely hot there wasn't too much water vapour in the air (which stops you from sweating out your excess heat). In 2006, at over 25%, the humidity was now proving to be a real killer - once a runner's cooling mechanism had been severely impaired, the heat literally cooked all of their internal organs, their brain included. The taller, thinner runners stood a better chance as their bodies were more able to radiate the heat - but the shorter and bigger runners resembled 'boil in the bag' meals.

We were literally stepping over people that had passed out on the floor. Some were fitting. And I mean proper rigour fits like you'd see if they were having an epileptic fit. One lady from Finland was doing just that with a Japanese camera crew just stood there filming her. Incredulously, not only were they not helping but they were actually shouting, 'You scleam louder! You scleam louder!' It was a complete bloody nightmare for her! I had actually spoken to her on registration day and her English was perfect. Bizarrely, after her recovery in the race infirmary, she'd lost her ability to speak her mother tongue and it was days before she could speak Finnish again.

One of the rules of the MdS is that every competitor must carry a distress flare. In 2006, each stage became more and more like Bonfire Night with very few minutes passing between flare releases summoning medical assistance and help. Everyone was destroyed by the end of Day Two - the MdS had reached its safety limit.

Then came Day Three…

Between the first two checkpoints I overestimated how far I'd run - the route began across a flat, dried out sandy river bed where the sun beat down on your head making you overheat. There was a fantastic heat haze in front of you as you looked across the surface of the $50^0+$ cauldron. If you ran too hard you'd burn up, if you ran too slowly you'd be totally sapped of energy and wouldn't recover. In all honesty you were sort of buggered either way. All you could do was traverse it as quickly as possible with your mind in one piece and your body and soul intact. You really were playing Russian Roulette with your life.

Next I reached a more technical part of the route where we were directed over some mini jebels (mountains) which were 200-300 metre climbs. The only thing was that I had totally run out of water - I'd drunk the lot. Now I was in trouble, 'Shit,' I thought, 'I've still got another maybe two or three kilometres to go and I'm as dry as a bone.' I couldn't see the next checkpoint and no-one around me had any water either.

I finally reached the checkpoint completely parched. The 1.5 litre bottle of water I was given didn't touch the sides and I asked for another despite the one hour time penalty I knew I'd incur for doing so. The lovely checkpoint crew were trying to discourage me, 'Rory - no, no, no. You will be ill.' All I said was, 'I don't care - just give me another bottle of water!'

Then I found my oasis in this giant, unforgiving landscape - some shade provided by three Land Rovers where I just sat and contemplated my predicament for 45 minutes. Psychologically I was in a total mess. I just thought, 'What's happened? I'm sure the last time I was here it was a piece of cake. Rory Coleman doesn't worry about doing the MdS. I'm a proven Desert Warrior.'

I'd found out the hard way that I wasn't. With a bucket of hindsight you only remember the good times and Patrick Bauer (Race Director) had turned his amps up to 11. Why? He wanted 'The World's Toughest Footrace' to be just that, renowned for being super-tough. He was a proud Frenchman wanting to make a statement, so in 2006 he'd upped the ante.

The 2006 race wasn't just the MdS - it had become the MdS squared! I simply hadn't expected it. I had thought it was, 'just another MdS.' I'd become so blasé about the race that I believed I could go and complete it with a certain amount of ease whenever I wanted to.

In the shade of the Land Rovers, blown away, I gathered my thoughts and very quickly learned how to rehydrate using the proper amount of salt in my water. The doctors were actually talking about going on strike because they were fixing people only for them to go back out the next day and place themselves into another life-threatening situation. You'd see people cross the line at death's door only to emerge from the race infirmary a few hours and five or six bags of IV fluid later, bouncing across the race bivouac like spring lambs. The doctors weren't happy about that one bit.

Before the last checkpoint there was a guy who had passed out and was in big trouble with a body temperature of around 42°C. Luckily, and I mean luckily, he'd been found by a female German competitor who'd previously won the MdS and understood how much trouble he was in. She immediately set off her flare to signal for an emergency helicopter pick-up. The doctors were certain he was going to die. Luckily for him he didn't but it was very much touch and go. He went back a couple of years later and this time he finished the race. That's the type of competitor that this race attracts.

Thankfully there has always been impressive medical care at the MdS - they are able to cope with virtually any medical emergency right there in the desert. The thing that drives people over the edge with this particular event is the prospect of not finishing and returning home on a plane full of hundreds of people wearing their medals and 'Finisher' t-shirts. How do you face your family and friends? Sadly, every year around 10% of those starting the MdS don't finish.

I was, and have always been, a starter-completer so this simply wasn't an option. Nonetheless I was totally destroyed - it felt like I'd been through a human washing machine. But it didn't matter how I felt as I knew I had to get up and do it again the next day and the next whether I liked it or not. I knew I had to break the race down into bite-sized chunks and just get from one checkpoint to the next.

Despite managing to complete the MdS in 2006, I suddenly realised that I couldn't wing it anymore. The first time I took part I'd run 86 marathons that year - I was incredibly fit. A few years before the 2006 event I'd run from London to Lisbon in Portugal and thought I was fit, but this was a real wake-up call - the biggest ever kick in the bollocks. This was pure Rory Coleman kryptonite. It was totally corrosive. It undermined my thoughts about what I was doing. I suddenly thought, 'This is Hard.' The race had now transformed itself from being a jolly run in the sand to a life or death experience.

A French competitor died the year afterwards.

Indeed, the thing which sets the more extreme ultra-marathons apart from your average London Marathon is that you do have to consider the risk of taking part. For example, if I take part in the Grand Union Canal Race (GUCR) - 145 miles down a canal towpath in the UK - what is the possibility of me meeting my maker along the way? Well I suppose I could fall into the water, I could have a heart attack - who knows - but there is a risk. On this particular event, the medical cover is a call to 999 - there's no helicopter to get you out of danger. It's 'risky' and 'hard' but not like the MdS - the MdS is in a dimension all of its own.

I've taken part in the GUCR three times now and standing in Gas Street Basin, Birmingham at 6:00am waiting to set off to run 145 miles 706 yards to Little Venice in London takes real balls. If I'd thought about running the 145 miles in one go I'm not sure I would have ever started as it's just a colossal distance which gradually wrecks your body over the course of nearly two days of running.

The race takes place on the second May Bank Holiday when it *always* rains - usually for the duration of the race and mostly torrential in my experience. I suppose it is a May Bank Holiday in Britain - what do you expect? Anyway, halfway through my first GUCR in 1999, the sole of my left foot fell off. Virtually half of my foot de-gloved leaving red raw skin. It wasn't fun when at 70 miles I was sat down looking at my foot's skin which was just flapping around in the wind.

When I ran it felt like I had red hot needles sticking into my foot every time I took a step; when I stopped it didn't ease. I still had

74 miles to go and I was ninth in the race. I knew I had to get on with it and keep going - after all it couldn't get any worse, could it?

The truth was that my feet had been drenched in the rain and because this was early on in my running career, I'd been wearing the wrong sock and shoe combination. The constant rubbing had melted the sole of my foot clean away. My sister and her husband were crewing for me which was great for supplies and morale, but it just kept on raining. I sheltered under a bridge for at least 45 minutes hoping it would stop. The thunder and lightning was all around me - one of the competitors actually got struck by lightning that year but luckily for her she lived to tell the tale.

Finally the rain relented and I got going again, proudly still maintaining my ninth position. After a while the pain didn't get any worse. The endorphins kicked in and my foot finally went numb until I stopped for a sleep - this was back in the days when you could stop during the race for 40 winks - so I got my head down for a couple of hours. Luckily, my crew had pitched a tent on a pub lawn on the banks of the canal in Milton Keynes. I laid in it in just my shorts - the steam literally coming off my body like a boiling kettle that then filled the tent. It was like sleeping in a Turkish Bath. My foot was on fire.

The best part was, I went to bed in ninth place and I woke up in sixth as some competitors had dropped out during the night. 'Well, that's a result!' I thought. 'Milton Keynes is a hell of a long way from Birmingham, especially when it's been lashing it down and I'm completely destroyed, but this is it - this is my race. This is the race where I find out just how long I can hit my head against a brick wall for before stopping!' Loads of people would have just given up, wouldn't they? Not me, though. I wanted to do as well as I possibly could, because I wanted to prove to myself that I'd become different.

I ventured on and eventually caught site of three guys running together ahead of me - I was slowly catching them. At every checkpoint I was told how far ahead of me they were, and at every turn or bend in the last few miles of the race I hoped I'd see them. Eventually I caught them - one of them had passed out, exhausted, another looked up and simply said, 'You bastard - we've been waiting for you.' I didn't stop to argue and I passed them like a 400 metre runner in full flight. I thought, 'At this rate I'm going to finish third in the race.' And for me - a heavy ex-drinker/smoker - I didn't care about my foot. I just thought, 'This is it - I've finally made the podium, I've found my thing.'

Had I been stalking them? Of course I had - for hours - and in that race I'd found my heaven amidst all of that hell.

But fast-forwarding to the MdS 2006, the GUCR was nothing compared to the hell of the Sahara. At that 2006 MdS, it was like they had the grill pan on full and they were blasting us with flame throwers whilst rubbing Napalm in our faces and kicking us constantly in the balls. The 13 litres of water allocated to us each day didn't quench the fire. It takes a lot to drink the equivalent of 26 x 500ml bottles of water in a day but it still wasn't enough to rehydrate me in the shade of those Land Rovers. I think that was the day when I grew up and thought, 'Why on earth am I putting myself through all of this?'

Until then I had felt like I could get through anything - even when I lost the bottom of my foot on the GUCR. I had coped with all of that, but I still needed to be taken to my limits.

It's like driving a fast car and seeing just how fast it can go. I still needed to find out who I really was. It's extremely important to me that I leave an epitaph on my tombstone saying, 'This is me - this is who I am.' I know I won't be here to see it, but my accomplishments will be there for others to see and hopefully to be inspired by.

I want people to know who I am.
I'm the person that does extraordinary stuff.
I'm Britain's Most Extreme Runner...

# CHAPTER ONE

## THE EARLY YEARS

### SHEEP - PINK FLOYD 1977

*I must have played this song a thousand times and it's my all-time 'Floyd Favourite'. Roger Waters' vitriolic lyrics describe the worst trait ever - being a 'Sheep', being someone that follows someone else's path and goes with the flock instead of being prepared to 'Stick Out' from the crowd. I've looked out over Jordan, just like the lyrics say, and the Psalm 23 parody is just priceless. The creativity of each phase of the 10 minute track amazes me each and every time I listen to it. There's a great live version on the 'Wish You Were Here' remastered album from 1974 ('Raving & Drooling') which is well worth a listen. The drive and ambition I've gained from this track over the years has been immense and I don't think songs gets much better than this one. Remember, 'Get out of the road, if you want to grow old.' It's a great adage.*

On paper I've had the opportunity to do some amazing things.

I've run nearly 1,000 marathons and over 200 ultra-marathons, completed the world's toughest foot race in the Sahara Desert - the Marathon des Sables - 13 times, broken nine different Guinness World Records for long-distance running, raced in Jordan from Amman to Petra without a map or compass along goat tracks and up remote mountains, and I once covered a 20th of the world's circumference in 43 days straight, running 31 miles each day.

I've also crossed the Atacama Desert in South America in locations so remote that if you broke your leg whilst running, you'd die; I've run a marathon between each and every one of the Premier League football clubs in Britain - meeting Sir Bobby Charlton along the way and shaking Alan Shearer's hand at the end - and I've run 145 miles along the Grand Union Canal from Birmingham to London - the running equivalent of banging your head against a brick wall and seeing who can last the longest. On that occasion it was me, although it was a very painful 38 hours and 9 minutes.

With 22 years of running under my belt, I'm now considered by many running publications, athletes and pundits to be one of the world's leading long-distance running coaches. I spend many a day meeting clients who, like me all those years ago, are trying to work out who they really are. Most want to change their lifestyles and find out what life is all about. I get lots of mid-life crises coming to see me who've realised that the big job doesn't interest them anymore - mainly men as they see themselves as empire builders. They want The Big Job, they desire money and respect and want to drive a team of people and ultimately be The Big Boss. When they reach the age of 40 they just decide, 'Bugger this, all I want is an easy life!' It's a bit like the 'When Harry Met Sally' scenario - people say to me, 'Err, I want what you've got.'

In fact, lots of people I coach tell me that I've got the best job in the world: the chance to spend my days out in the open, running and exploring. I think people look at me and think, 'He looks like a pretty happy sort of dude.' And they're right. I am happy. And I'm also happy to fast track those people I meet so that they can learn from my running trials and tribulations too.

Behind my personal triumphs lie some harsh truths that I'm going to finally face up to in this book - as catharsis for me and perhaps as a demonstration to you, the reader, of how far us humans can go when we decide to set our minds on a new goal and pull ourselves out of our self-imposed mess.

The truth is, running saved me from a lifetime of obesity, alcoholism and a 40-a-day cigarette smoking addiction. Uncertain of where my life was going by the age of 30, I was lost and in complete freefall. My older brother, a talented GP, even told me I was facing death by the age of 40 if I continued the way I was going. So I finally did something about my addictions - I was determined to change and I started afresh - it was a sort of rebirth.

Despite everything I've achieved since making that life-transforming decision, it's been a rocky road to get here. My stubbornness, perseverance and dogged determination - admittedly not always the most appealing of characteristics - have got me to where I am today. I've always had the desire to be different, to stand out from the crowd, just like so many of my clients who come to see me looking for change. I think this desire has been an integral part of who I am from a very early age. It's rooted deeply in my upbringing, my family, my generation, my experiences - sometimes troubled - in my earlier years, my hours of emotional hill-climbing. These have all made me the individual I am today…

I am a child of the sixties, born in 1962 to good parents who raised me in a tied-cottage on a farm in a place called Luddington. It's a lovely, picture box village near Stratford-upon-Avon in Warwickshire. My Dad had also grown up on his Dad's farm where he later worked after WWII. He left school to start work when he was just 14 but got paid very little and throughout my childhood Dad didn't earn very much. My Mum stayed at home to look after my brother, sister and me which meant we struggled to make ends meet. Nevertheless, I lived in a happy environment with loving parents who loved and still love each other after 60 years of marriage.

My Doctor Brother is three years older than me and over

the last 30 years he's become a very successful GP. He must have got his smarts from my mum who is also very clever - in fact she's a very bright lady indeed.

It's her relationship with my Dad that's truly unique. After 60 years of marriage they still walk around the supermarket holding hands. They're the best of friends. They're not interested in other people - only each other. It's their world. When something happens to one of them I don't know what will happen as they are such a strong partnership and have set me such an amazing example over the years.

Still, it wasn't all easy going. When I was little I just couldn't get the talking thing and didn't talk properly until I was five. No matter how hard I tried I couldn't master the concept of speech and how to do it. I'd miss the first letters off all of my words. I would say, 'ello, my 'ame is 'ory 'oleman...' In fact I'd talk such gobbledygook that my parents would ask my brother what I was saying and he would translate it for them.

I must be on the Asperger's spectrum or something, but whatever the cause it still impacts the way I speak now. When I speak, you can hear me pronounce every single syllable. It's because I ended up having to be taught by a speech therapist to speak correctly. Miss Beckett was her name and she was new to her job - she was very patient and I remember sitting on her knee for hours as a small child working on my speech. After a few weeks I'd got it and have never looked back since.

Not that any of this helped when I got to school. During the six weeks I spent going to speech therapy classes once a week, my teachers still struggled with my word blindness. They would even say, 'If his speech doesn't improve then he won't be able to stay at this school.'

The thing is, my Dad had the same speech issues. In fact, he was six - a year older than me - by the time he had finally learned how to speak properly. I seemed to inherit the problem.

On the plus side, it was a very character-building experience and really laid the foundations of who I am today. I'll either completely grasp an idea or concept, or not comprehend it at all. I find that things can confuse me or just pass me by.

For example, a client of mine recently bought me, very kindly, a digital fitness wristband device. It wasn't working, so the manufacturers sent me a 20-step manual on how to reboot it - 'Press this button; delete that; install that.' I had to 'phone the manufacturer's helpline as my brain just couldn't compute the mass of written information. I'm definitely much more of a pictorial person.

But there is a positive side to being like this, especially where my running is concerned. My confidence in my ability to run across the Sahara Desert, for example, has stemmed from being completely self-taught. All of the knowledge I have acquired, both physical and technical, to enable me to complete the race successfully, safely and efficiently has come from hard graft and personal investment. It's the same when I do any big running events like that - my strength comes from the fact that I've done all of my own 'tried and tested' research. I know it works and I'm completely in control behind the steering wheel.

It probably makes me a bit of a sociopath if I'm being honest. I like to be in control and make all the rules. I can give a lecture on my own personal experiences of running extreme events like the MdS to hundreds of people at an Expo, no worries. I'd completely love every single moment of it. But if you gave me a script to remember in front of all those people, I just wouldn't be able to do it. I wouldn't be able to learn or retain any of it.

I knew everybody that lived in Luddington village by the time I was seven. I can actually still name all of the houses and all of the residents. At the time, they all seemed really old - I expect they were probably only in their early fifties, as I am now. In fact, some of them are still alive and still live there and still look the same.

There weren't too many playmates in the village though. Out of maybe 100 houses there were a dozen kids - not many, is it? So if you fell out with friends as a child... you were pretty lonely. It was so innocent though and during those years you could play football on the road outside our house because there weren't that many cars. It's totally unthinkable now of course. We had a 'phone box opposite our house which had an old Welford-on-Avon dialling code - its number was Welford-on-Avon 361. If the 'phone rang when you were nearby you'd answer it and say, 'Who's calling? Who are you after?' Then you'd go and knock on their door and tell them that somebody wanted them on the 'phone. We didn't have a home 'phone for years - we didn't have a colour TV, either. It was quite a meagre existence actually and because my sister hadn't been born at that stage, Sunday night was 'bath night' and meant that, as the youngest, I'd be last in the bath. That's the way it went.

I followed in my brother's footsteps and passed my 11+. This enabled me to go to King Edward VI Grammar School for Boys in Stratford-upon-Avon - the very one Shakespeare had attended back in the Sixteenth Century. It was a real privilege as it was, and still is, one of the top secondary schools in the country. Having an elder brother there meant he could help me with my homework and defend me if I got into trouble.

At 10 years old, I remember looking at my brother and all the other kids coming out of school and thinking how lucky they were. They looked so smart and clever. I was worried that I wouldn't be able to pass my 11+ and go there, especially as I didn't want to disappoint my parents who were only too aware of the value of a grammar school education. Maybe I was a borderline case and because my brother was already there, they let me in too. I'll never know, but it did make me value the education and I loved that school.

What really fired me up was that the teachers treated us like we were in the army. It was extremely regimented. You were taught to have a lot of respect. If you answered the teachers back, you knew what was coming. In those days they believed in corporal punishment and they could dish it out at any time, without reserve. The teachers were also very clever and easily deserved the respect they demanded. For example, during our first lesson with my physics teacher, Dr. D. G. A. Dyson, we were handed out our textbooks only for us to discover that he was the author. That was super-cool in my mind - what a clever guy. Yes it did feel at times like we were prisoners in Colditz but that was part of the game.

It was a game too as amongst 400 bright boys, if a teacher was rubbish they were soon found out. They'd have a really tough time because kids can be hard work. We had one rare female teacher, Mrs Pyott, who didn't last long. She immediately became 'Mrs Ryott' and from that moment on she was a goner. On the other hand, there was a maths teacher who could do logarithms in his head and draw a perfect circle on the blackboard without a blackboard compass, plus he was as hard as nails. When he did this stuff, I just thought, 'Wow.' Understanding Latin, however, forget it. Although I speak French pretty well now, thanks to all the running races and running-related work I've done, back then I just couldn't process the written language. Today I'm someone who'll have a go at anything and would probably do a lot better, but the study of languages back then was a real stumbling block.

Part of the problem may have been that at primary school I'd grown up feeling like a maverick, like my own person. I really loved it. We played sport, we went to science clubs. They were my Halcyon days. We were growing up in the space age. Space travel was the big thing. Neil Armstrong landed on the moon on 20th July, 1969. I remember that date so clearly - the defining moment of mankind's history in the 20th century. I'd been in Wolverhampton during the day visiting my Great Uncle and Aunts, and I was woken up to see 'Man walk on the Moon'. I loved it. The sense of exploration really gripped me. I thought, 'That's where we're all going to go - we're all going to fly around in spaceships.' I thought that life was going to be some kind of cosmic existence.

The interesting thing was that at my secondary school we weren't graded A, B, C, etc.; we were graded 1 to 29, the number of boys in my class. First being brilliant and 29th being rubbish, even though you could have achieved a good mark in the subject. It was your position that really mattered. It was all about being first. I liked that as I was first in art, woodwork and the creative subjects - this meant I didn't get worried if I underperformed in one of the other subjects - I had made my mark. When I sat my 11+ I didn't lose any sleep the night before. I just went into the exam, answered the questions and got through. I did the same for my O-levels and A-levels.

As in most schools, if your appearance diverged from the norm you were an easy target. There were two such targets in my year - one really thin and the other really fat - both of whom got picked on every day because they stood out from the crowd. I quickly learnt that there were two ways to get through school unscathed - you could either melt into the crowd or you could excel at something. I was lucky enough to excel at art - I was frequently called a 'fantastic artist'. Obviously the complements were rewarding enough in themselves, but what made them even more valuable is that they enabled me to just sail through school - I had a new identity - I was the Class Artist.

I was also a crowd-pleaser - one of the class fools that did uncomplimentary impersonations of teachers behind their backs to make the other kids laugh, and ultimately I suppose to make them like me. Maybe it was because I wanted to please others, to fit in, to be liked by my peer group. I think deep down I'm a real Show Pony, I've just got that kind of personality. That's why my current email signature lists the near 1,000 marathons I've run plus my Guinness World Records. I'm like, 'TA-DA!

THIS IS ME!' But I've come to believe that, actually, we're all trying to chip away at our headstones, write our own epitaphs and make our marks on this world - aren't we? Otherwise, why are we here?

I was very sporty when I was young and I played County-level cricket. I was even invited to trials for Warwickshire and was awarded a cricketing scholarship when I was 13. I batted against England's Gladstone Small - the guy with no neck. We even called him 'No Neck'. We took no prisoners. Neither did he - he was a ferociously aggressive bowler even then. The day I carted him for a few fours was the highlight of my cricketing career and is my cricketing claim to fame. It felt good!

Oddly, given the extra-long running distances I'm now more noted for, I also did the school cross country run but I can't say I really enjoyed it. It was every Friday afternoon in the mud and rain each spring term. Without any specific training, I finished about 10th out of 29 kids which was no good for me. To be the Class Athlete I needed to be first. Cross country just wasn't far enough for me to make my mark so it became a definite no-go zone.

My school produced confident young men with a hint of arrogance. In an ID parade I reckon I could pick out those who'd been there. They'd gone to the school based on merit, not because their parents had paid for them to be there.

It's funny - we had a class reunion when we were 40 and I met all these people I hadn't seen for 20 years. They all seemed really downhearted about how their lives had panned out. Some of them divulged that they'd actually hated school, a fact that I was blissfully unaware of at the time because I had loved it! I'd loved that environment. It wasn't a picnic every day of course. You could certainly get challenged and bullied and there would be tough situations with teachers from time to time. Nonetheless, my overwhelming memory of school life is one of happiness and fulfilment.

It was around that time that my fascination with music really peaked. When I was five there had been a really hot summer and 'Hole in my Shoe' by Traffic had reached number two in the charts. I just loved that song and quickly moved on to 'Yellow Submarine' by The Beatles. My discovery of glam rock a few years later was the icing on the cake. Sweet, Gary Glitter and Slade made Sunday evenings a real treat and it was all about listening to the latest Top 20 on Radio One armed with a cassette recorder and a microphone so I could record the music and then play back my favourite chart songs to death.

Then I heard Mike Oldfield's 'Tubular Bells' and Pink Floyd's 'Dark Side of the Moon' - these two albums gained a special place in my heart. They simply blew me away. The moment I heard Tubular Bells I was mesmerised. In fact it was the first record I ever bought, on 13th November, 1976; it's a pivotal date in my life. I had the same feeling when I heard Freddie Mercury of Queen... I just thought, 'This is bloody brilliant!' Nonetheless, when my brother gave me a copy of the Genesis album 'The Lamb Lies Down on Broadway' borrowed from one of his school-mates, I knew Genesis were going to be a life-long partner from that point on! Between us we quickly bought their entire back catalogue as well as played that album so many times the cassette tape went thin. The Lamb Lies Down on Broadway is at the top of my playlist. It's been with me for the best part of 40 years and it still feels as fresh as it did the day I first listened to it. It's timeless and I love it.

Life was all relatively plain sailing during my school years. The fact that I came from a small village, had been to an all-boys school, and had parents who weren't very well-off had left me with precious little real-life experience. After my A-levels I went to art school. I had led a pretty sheltered existence up until this point which meant that, as far as girls were concerned, I turned up at that institution like Dracula at a blood bank! It wasn't just the girls either - there were also cigarettes, soft drugs and booze... you didn't have to wear a uniform and you didn't have to turn up for lessons if you didn't want to.

I became a bit of a rebel. I convinced myself that my destiny was to become a photographer and started a photography degree only to quit soon afterwards as I just couldn't do it. I couldn't do the necessary reading and academic part of the course - it just wasn't me. I was great at taking the photographs and being creative but the rest of the degree left me cold and left the lecturers frustrated with me. I became frustrated with myself and spent more time in the university bar than in lectures. And from that point on, I became ill and depressed and by the end of the first year I thought, 'Oh fuck this, I'm jacking it in.'

Looking back, I was drunk the whole time. I wasn't like most students who have a few drinks; I would get seriously drunk, to the point that I eventually got hepatitis. I'd overlooked myself and my liver, which was now infected, and I was actually desperately unhappy. To make matters worse, I also had to tell everyone that I'd failed. I hated having to say that. I had to go back to my Mum and Dad and admit that they'd been right when they'd said I shouldn't have gone to university, that it wasn't right for me. But I'd gone and done it anyway. And now I'd cocked up, big time. Plus all my peers knew I'd failed. Even now it's hard to own up to my failure at further education and it's something I'm really embarrassed about because, in hindsight, I could have chosen a better path. Failure is something I have never been able to deal with very well.

After dropping out, I went back to stay with my parents for six months and simply did nothing. Instead, they both looked after me whilst I went through the motions of what to do with my life. This was when I met the woman who would later become my first wife. I was 20, she was a couple of years older than me, and it seemed like a good thing to get together. I got myself straight and we looked at moving in together as a couple. Back then you could buy a house on the cheap and we scraped together a deposit for a new build house in Stratford-upon-Avon.

To get the cash I went out and got numerous jobs working around the clock, seven days a week. These included working on an archaeological dig as an illustrator, drawing the various finds that the Warwickshire County Council archaeologists had found on their digs. I also went to work in a studio drawing Yellow Pages display adverts. I topped this up by working in Dixons, the camera shop. Having gained some experience of pasting up artwork, I quickly progressed and went to work for a couple of printing companies. I was a quick learner and from the age of 21, I worked my way up through the ranks of apprenticeship to the point where I was managing the day-to-day running of a print company by the time I was 28. That was my first taste of what it takes to manage and motivate people. There were two characteristics which I found really helped my cause - optimism and enthusiasm. These came very easily to me and they are two words that I'd like to think most folk that know me today would associate with me.

But behind all that success there lingered a few demons. At art school I'd taught myself how to smoke and persevered with it to fit in with my peers; I'd also continued to drink heavily. These habits helped me to fit in perfectly with the 'Print Game' and by the time I was 28, I was a 40 cigarettes-a-day man. A lot of business back then was undertaken in pubs. We'd have meetings and hand work over to clients over a few pints. In fact at one of the places I worked, if you didn't drink at least three or four pints in the pub at lunchtime then you were considered a bit of a 'Jessie'. I put on stacks of weight and when I looked at myself in the mirror I hated the person looking back at me.

To make matters worse, the woman I'd married and bought a house with didn't want the same things as me, and vice versa. After a couple of years I think she had decided that actually maybe I wasn't the person for her. But failure wasn't an option so, rather than call it a day, we found things to try to glue it all together.

In 1988 my eldest daughter was born when I was 26, next was my eldest son in 1990. So there I was: a guy with two young children and an unhappy wife at home not liking it when I came home tired and tipsy. It was like, 'Shall I go home or go to the pub? Hmm, maybe I'll go to the pub because I'll be in the shit when I get home,' and then that just became the daily ritual. There were lots of other 'Five O'Clock Club' members to drink with and there was a lot of male chauvinism and bravado in staying at the bar and not going home to face the music.

My weekend drinking was just as bad. Sunday was fun-day - at midday I'd go down to the off-license and buy a four pack of Stella and when it opened again at seven o'clock, I'd go and buy four more. I felt like I was a party guy and proud of my ability to knock back strong lager. But it wasn't good. I started getting into more and more scrapes, each one worse than the last, and finding myself in bad situations - drunk behind the wheel of a car, drunk in a club. I spent hours down the pub when I should have been at home with my wife and children.

By this stage I looked like shit. I was 15 stone; I had a muffin top fold of fat over the top of my 36-inch waist jeans. I had a beard, I had long hair and I hated myself. I couldn't believe I'd let myself get into that kind of shape. I've had clients who say, 'I'm 25 stone and I've got to lose weight.' I think, 'Well why didn't you address the situation when you hit 20 stone?' We can become so blind to the elephant in the room - I did just that and very soon I was circling the drain. My mind-set was ridiculously distorted. I felt that as long as I worked hard and had enough money to pay the bills and feed my ever increasing habits, life was rich.

What a Pratt!

But that's the way my mind worked. My standards hit an all-time low. No wonder my wife didn't want me. I knew that and thought, 'Bugger it, why bother? I'll have another drink. Why bother making myself buy trendy clothes, why bother how I look, why go to the gym? What difference would it make to a miserable home life?'

The problem was that I wanted to get out of the situation but actually I wasn't brave enough to do it. I'd become a really weak-willed person. I'd been 'energy-vampired'; I'd had my enthusiasm sucked out of me. Everything had gone so wrong and I felt totally lost in life.

I knew I'd have to do something about it. But it's really difficult at the time as you have to pluck up courage and you've got to go against all your values. You've also got to go against your peer group and fight the negativity of those people saying, 'You'll never give it up!' You've got to swim against the tide and fight, fight for your life.

Our marriage lasted until 1999 - 14 years. At the time, divorce was less prevalent and my parents had set me the benchmark for having a long marriage. Nonetheless, I felt that getting myself straight was more important than sorting out my home life - it proved to be a long process. This was the unhappiest period of my life so far and I just didn't know what I was doing. It's really difficult when you've lost your direction. My addictions were out of control and all the signs were there for an early exit.

But the thing that really pushed me over the edge to change was the realisation that I had been drunk every day of my youngest son's life - Sam was now six months old. It was very embarrassing. I vividly remember Christmas-time 1993 - there was a flu epidemic and I was coughing so much that I had to use an asthma inhaler to help me breathe. I was pneumonic, and yes I was still smoking! So on Boxing Day I decided that I would never smoke again. The Freddie Mercury tribute concert the previous year was still fresh in my mind - Freddie was dead and gone and I felt I was going to join him.

In a drunken state I just knew I had to do something to save myself from total self-destruction, so I cried for help - I 'phoned the Samaritans. Back then there weren't the counselling facilities that we have today and I didn't think about going to see my GP. I would have been too embarrassed to talk to my brother because he would just say, 'Well I told you so,' and I didn't want to disappoint my parents by admitting I had a massive problem. I couldn't talk to my wife because she had totally lost interest in me.

But when I 'phoned the Samaritans, they suggested I call Alcoholics Anonymous. That was a really depressing thought. I didn't want to sit in a circle and admit defeat by telling people I was an alcoholic failure. I just thought, 'I'll go and fix myself.'

So, after the Christmas break, I went straight home from work instead of going straight to the pub. My idea wasn't to run nearly 1,000 marathons. It wasn't to run thousands of miles. I didn't know anything about running. All I thought was, I've got to clean up my act and, wanting to lose weight, I stood on the scales... I was 95 kilos (15 stone), even if I stood on one leg. I was flabbergasted. My only thought was, 'Well runners - they're thin. They're lean and mean looking people - I know, I'll go for a run.'

And so, still dressed in my work clothes - trousers, a puffer jacket, my Clarks leather shoes... I went for a run...

# CHAPTER TWO

## KICKING THE HABIT

SECRET WORLD (LIVE) - PETER GABRIEL 1992

*As an all-time hero of mine, this track encompasses everything that is simply brilliant about Gabriel's music. I somehow missed the original on his 'US' album and the subsequent tour, much to my dismay. On first hearing, this was an instant hit for me and the 'Live' version has a slight edge over the studio recording in my opinion. Having lived in many different 'Secret Worlds' during my lifetime the 'Breaking it Up, Shaking it Up' reflects the many regenerations I've been through. I love the gentle build and crescendo of the track and Gabriel's vocals in both low and high range are really powerful.*

As simple as 'just going for a run' sounds, it hadn't been a walk in the park to get to that point in my life. It was Wednesday 5th January, 1994 - the first day back at work after Christmas. For the whole day, all I'd been thinking about was going for that first fledgling run. I'd been contemplating change for some time now but finally the penny had dropped.

I'd reached a new low-point in my life journey which I now call my 'Point Zero'. My thoughts were, 'Right, this is my day! Bugger the pub - I'm doing something to change my situation.' By the time I got home from work I was fixated with the idea.

So the moment I got through the front door I stood on the scales, looked down and thought, 'Bloody hell! I'm 15 stone!' Don't get me wrong, I was prepared for a bit of a shock - I was physically uncomfortable from being overweight and hated that feeling. Inside I felt toxic, like the toxicity was inside the DNA of my skin. But 15 stone! That's 95 kilos...

The surprise also came from the fact that I hid my body fat pretty well, spreading it neatly around my body rather than having it all in one place. Sure, I was a bit chubby in the face, and I had a beer belly, but that was acceptable down at the pub. I was a drinker - it was a trademark, a kind of badge of honour.

But seeing that I weighed 15 stone on the scales immediately spurred me into action. I knew I wanted to get rid of it. I'd managed to lose a bit of weight in the past so I knew that if I set my mind to it I could do it. It was definitely a turning of the tide, and such a momentous occasion that every year since, on that exact date, I've posted myself a children's birthday card to celebrate and to congratulate myself on spending another year dry... another year of being 'a new me'... a reaffirmation that drinking is no longer a part of my life and a reminder never to embrace it again.

Between the ages of 21 and 31, aside from the births of my children, I had been very unhappy. On that day, I had a rebirth and developed a whole new persona. I realised that I couldn't change the past but I could change the future and lock the old me away in a vault. My 22nd Birthday card this year felt very satisfying. No-one else sent me one as that day is only of real significance to me.

This whole transformation has had a major impact on my career as a coach because I can draw on my own past to help my clients. One lady I'm currently coaching has now been dry for eight weeks and she's using the same techniques that I used back then to overcome her addiction. I've simplified it now, it goes like this - you replace three behavioural traits about yourself that you don't like (mine were - I was a drunk, I smoked and I ate a very poor diet) with three habits you'll be proud of.

In 1994 I stopped drinking, I stopped smoking and I went on a rather unscientific 500-calorie-a-day diet, eating only a ham sandwich and three cream crackers a day. I knew I had to lose three stone and, of course, without a lot of calories going in the weight just dropped off and I quickly saw the results. I felt euphoric! I also decided that I would immediately replace one of my bad habits - going to the pub every evening after work - with running, for the same time slot.

Likewise, I replaced my smoking habit with a newfound determination to clean up my act. I cut my long, shoulder-length hair. I shaved off my beard which had been a mask for me to hide behind - a kind of cloaking device. I bought some new clothes to stop me looking like a tramp. I took my entire record collection to a second-hand shop and disposed of it - to me, all that music represented all the bad things about my life up until then - all the scrapes I'd gotten into when drunk. All those Genesis, Pink Floyd, U2 and Yes albums - they all went. They'd been the soundtrack to a very unhappy, dysfunctional life. They just had to go.

So in my work clothes and my Clarks shoes I stepped out of the door and off I went. But because I was so keen to get going, I shot off far too quickly! I hadn't warmed up and my running technique in the Clarks shoes left a lot to be desired. As a heavy smoker, my lungs were soon killing me. Having no idea what I was doing or where I was going, I found myself sat on the curb, wheezing, totally speechless after just 100 steps. I was amazed, embarrassed and flabbergasted at how unfit I was.

Nevertheless, this didn't make me feel downhearted. Instead the experience had given me a deep sense of hope and motivation. When I got back home I even weighed myself, trying not to be too disappointed that the scales still said 15 stone. I felt inspired to try harder, to run further the next day, to repeat my new adventure into fitness. I knew immediately that running would be my path to salvation and a new life.

The following day, the distance doubled to a massive 200 steps. Unlike some people who start a journey of rebirth like this, I was adamant that I wouldn't begin with the best of intentions only to take my foot off the pedal. A lot of people get started, get fitter, lose the weight, stop drinking - but then something gets in the way or they get distracted and that's where the journey ends for them. For me, it became my 100% focus. Knowing it suited me, I became extremely determined that nothing would ever stop me... and it hasn't... 22 years later.

Within three months of embarking upon my exciting new lifestyle, a business I co-owned folded and my business partner and I parted company. We got rid of each other. He was a similar person to the old me - we had enabled each other to drink. Now we didn't go to the pub together and get drunk after a hard day's work we had nothing in common and cashed in our chips. Have I seen him since? Of course not. Is he still a drinker? I don't know. I haven't got a clue. He's locked in the vaults with the rest of my past. It sounds cruel but I was really determined! I had to leave that working-drinking-smoking scenario as getting better was my new priority. I'd reached the stage where I just had to look after number one.

Underlying this obsession of mine to stay focused, to not deviate, to maintain my tunnel vision, is the fact that I have never forgotten how important running is to me. Success is determined by the amount of effort you invest in something. Many of my clients are already determined to change when they contact me. They have aspirations - to lose weight, to get a new marathon PB or to run across the Sahara. They've already bought into and committed themselves to achieving their goal. So for me it's just about stoking their fires by enthusiastically reminding them how much success will mean to them when they achieve their end goal - that's how I have managed to retain my own focus all these years...

... And that's why I had such an affiliation with my first ever client. Like me, he was an alcoholic, only he would drink three bottles of wine a day. He's been dry ever since I spent that month working with him, but back then he was someone who would black out whilst being drunk, occasionally whilst looking after his children. One day, in fact, one of his kid's teachers brought him home to his wife and said, 'Is this your husband as I think he's a bit tiddly?' He was paralytic.

His wife knew about my own transformation through a family friend and asked me to help. When I got to their house the place looked like a bomb-site. To make matters worse, he was sporting a massive black eye from passing out and hitting his head on the pavement.

My course of action was all-consuming - I completely took over his daily routine and started to clean him up. First, I told him to go upstairs and tidy himself up because he looked - and smelt - like a tramp. From then onwards, I would go to their house first thing every morning to get him out of bed, take him to the bus stop and put him on the bus to his work. With his wife's help, we put him into a very controlled situation where he was never on his own. They lived opposite a Tesco Express, so in the morning he'd buy three bottles of wine for a tenner. He'd drink one straight down, hide one in the hedge and take one to work for lunchtime. The bottle in the hedge would be drunk later that evening after supper on the pretence that he was going out for a walk.

In his new regime there was a curfew. He couldn't leave the house once he'd got home. There was a white line in the middle of the road between him and the Tesco Express which he wasn't allowed to cross. We just put in some really simple new rules for him to follow. It required real mental strength. We did do some running together but more as a distraction from the booze - he wasn't a runner. In fact, he's my only client who's ever put on weight and never run a race. But there's no question it changed his life. That said, if I met him in the street today he probably wouldn't acknowledge me, I understand that. I'm his past you see, something he wants to forget. That's fine, I'm cool with that. I was his catalyst. I was Person X that took him from one place to another.

I've seen his wife since and she's so grateful because she's got her old husband back, the man she fell in love with. Did I have much empathy with him during the process because of my own past with drinking? Not a lot. Actually I was pretty harsh on him - he was at Point Zero and needed my discipline.

This was when I realised I had found my calling in life - all of that time spent drinking and smoking hadn't been wasted after all - my personal experience gave me a unique skill that enabled me to help people in a way very few others would be able. At 31 I had taken control, I had decided I wanted at least another 60+ years on Planet Earth, I had decided what the New Improved Rory Coleman was going to do, what he was going to look like. I had decided that the new Rory Coleman wasn't going to drink anymore, was going to tidy himself up and get rid of all the negativity that was messing him up. I had a revelation and thought, 'I can turn it all into a positive, I can help other people going through something similar and I can earn a living at the same time.'

When I started my own journey towards a healthier lifestyle back in January 1994 it was Uber Serious - I knew this was my Last Chance Saloon. Soon I'd be kicked out of home, live in a cardboard box and drink meths for a living. I felt I was facing certain death. So I was, really, very lucky indeed - I knew with absolute certainty what had to happen to me, what was going to happen to me, it felt inevitable. It was one hell of a nosedive and I managed to pull the plane up just before it hit the deck.

I've met loads of people who are heading that way. Going back to that lady I'm working with at the moment, I've helped her pull out of her own nosedive. And I'm not kidding - her landing gear scraped the ground she was that close. She had got into a habit of drinking whilst at work - one day she had run out of alcohol and she crashed her car whilst out driving to top up her supplies. Not good, is it? She was morbidly unhappy but her metamorphosis has been remarkable. She's in her mid-forties and has really turned a corner - she looks great now, really healthy. She just needed somebody to look out for her. She's been crying out for love for years, couldn't find it and discovered she could numb the pain with alcohol. I can relate to her predicament 100% as, at the slightest sign of trouble, I used to reach for another four-pack of Stella.

Once I started running, I didn't get that burning desire to drink. Same with the cigarettes - I just cut them out of my life. I had got to a stage where their toxicity was making me feel really ill. This coupled with the discovery that reversing the damage to your lungs from smoking is actually fairly quick gave me the impetus I needed to stick with it. Just 20 minutes after stubbing out my last cigarette I felt better. They say that if you can quit cigarettes for 28 days then you're five times more likely to permanently quit - and that really was the case with me. Alcohol and cigarettes are both kryptonite for me - they corrode my inner soul.

All of the people I used to meet in the pub were also immediately excluded from my life. I didn't want to see those people anymore. They were also corrosive - enabling me to drink and behave badly. Also when you go to the pub for an hour-and-a-half, you just talk a load of old bollocks, don't you? You talk about football and it's all men's talk, it doesn't go anywhere. And actually what you find out is that you talk about the same things with the same people every day and it's just inane drivel.

Of course back then I didn't set out to run marathons...

I just wanted to escape what I now refer to as my 'DFS Sofa' existence - a 'buy now, pay later' kind of life. You smoke and drink lots now and when you're 60 or 70, that's when it catches up with you - and we all know people, celebrities included, that it's caught up with don't we? It's not just about the damage it causes to your health either, it's about all those relationships you destroy in the process. My wife was pleased that I wasn't going to the pub and coming home drunk, but by that stage we were living parallel lives anyway. I'd probably been really awful to live with up until that point so we'd just sort of got into a rut - a stalemate. I am grateful to her though, that she didn't stand in the way of my early transformation.

In no time at all people began to notice a change in me. I'd lost three stone in a month! People would say, 'Wow, you look great!' and I would reply, 'Well, I've started running.' Yes, I'd become a proper runner. In fact I've since learnt that anyone of any age can become a runner and undergo a complete life transformation in just 12 weeks, I'm living proof of that.

I ran in my work clothes for about a month and then I went to a shop and bought some trainers. I didn't have a clue. By chance, the trainers I chose weren't too bad - I tested them out by running the school cross country course I hadn't really enjoyed when I was a kid. The first time I ran it I covered the 5km (3.1 miles) in 30 minutes. Not bad.

The distance just began to multiply… 100 steps… 200 steps… 400 steps… Actually, after a week I was probably running up to two miles, and then I remember I completed a 10 miler a month later. I thought I'd better do this 10-mile training run before the Stratford Half Marathon I'd entered. After that, I wanted to go longer - I'd seen the London Marathon on TV every year and that was going to be my next big goal. That was what I would build up to next. I couldn't get in in 1994 so I aimed for 1995 - I got a ballot place and booked my first 'London' for 2nd April, 1995.

Before long my training runs were getting longer - between 3 and 7 miles a day. The weight was falling off me and I absolutely loved it.

I was injury-free and have been to this day. I've been very lucky. I think my physical hardiness must have something to do with me coming into running late. At 31, my body had already fossilised and fused. I wasn't running all that fast so I didn't put loads of different stresses and strains on my body either. Biomechanically I'm very, very lucky, plus I've developed a very energy-efficient running style - if you watch me run I've got a very low leg lift. I've also always worn really good trainers by well-researched brands.

I went to a running shop when I first started called The Birmingham Runner. A guy in there called Dave Jones took a bit of a shine to me - he could see I was enthusiastic. I used to go and see him and he'd show me which shoes he thought were the best for my running style. He was absolutely spot-on, so I must thank him for that - in those shoes I would run through all weather conditions no matter what.

With running, I just had to go and do it. It just became a regular daily part of my life. It gave me a state of mind where all I had to worry about was my next step. It isolated me from all of my problems so no matter what was happening at work, at home, with the tax man, whatever - it was all parked up in one place. That's what I really loved the most about running - the pure escapism.

My life was in complete turmoil - I'd messed it up for the past 10 years - but at least I could go running which was really positive. I was starting to achieve things... one Saturday morning I ran 13 miles. For me that was something else and in April 1994 I ran the Stratford Half Marathon - it was awesome.

What I loved about the Stratford Half Marathon was that it went through the village where I'd lived for the whole of my childhood. It was tradition for all the locals to come out of their houses and watch the race flow through the village. Since the early eighties I had joined them, standing in my parents' garden with a B&H in one hand and a pint of Stella in the other saying, 'Silly sods.'

This was in the early years of marathon running in the UK. My parents' old house was at the '4 Mile' mark and then the '17 Mile' mark of the two lapped course. People regularly passed out on the bank of grass in front of their garden. It was a prime location for runners to hit 'the wall' on seeing the hill out of the village coupled with the 17 Mile marker next to some lovely grass to lie down on - it was most amusing for us onlookers. The ambulance would be parked beside their gate and there would be some very tired runners being administered first aid and being wrapped up in silver blankets. We'd stand there and just go, 'Oh, look at that,' and take the piss.

But this year was different - some 10 years later I was actually running it myself... with my head held high... with all the villagers watching me - it was such a positive experience. In years gone by I'd actually, secretly, been envious of the marathoners but now I was one of them. I felt part of the running groovy gang!

These days I'm often the one getting abuse, both when I'm training and racing. I've had people virtually shouting down my ear when I'm running and it has frightened the living daylights out of me! That's life I suppose - maybe it's jealousy on their part, like it probably was for me back then, and in their heart of hearts they wish they were running too. When you're out on the road, running along, you can look - and feel - pretty vulnerable. There's a fragility that I find some people are keen to abuse. Horn beeping, shouting and getting sprayed by cars deliberately driving through close-by puddles are all part of the 'joys' of road-running! People love to pick on those more vulnerable than themselves - particularly when they are being cheered on by other passengers and can hide behind the mask of their car.

That's why, for my first month of running, I ran in my work clothes in the dark. I'd come home and just go and run in my jeans. I did get a bit sweaty, but it was January and we don't live in the warmest of climes, do we? Since I didn't know where this running was taking me, or if I'd even last the week, it felt a bit premature to go and buy some proper gear. I was still running when February came along so I treated myself to a pair of tracksuit bottoms - I ran in these and a sweatshirt. I still didn't have any running apparel because I wasn't a runner. I was just doing something I thought I should do. There weren't any running websites I could look at and I didn't know of any 'How to Run' books so I just carried on doing what I was doing.

Answering that call to run had saved me, no question. If I hadn't gone running on 5th January, 1994 I wouldn't be here now. It was a momentary decision that saved my life. I'd played sport in the past but given it up - when I was 18 I decided that actually it was more fun to go to the pub than to play cricket. At one time I played a lot of squash - I quit that at university. I was now quitting my marriage.

But running fitted my personality. I fully accept that I'm not a team player. Yes, I could play cricket as long as I was either batting or bowling, but I didn't really get the camaraderie bit in between. Cricket wasn't like football where there are 11 of you playing a game, passing a ball around, depending on each other and working closely together, as a team, to win. I think it goes back to my childhood. I spent a lot of time playing on my own as a young child and I was completely happy with that. Even now I need time on my own. I need time to do the things I want to do and I don't want to be interrupted - it's my free-time when I zone out and I find it easy to amuse myself. I hear folk sometimes say that they're bored - I've never ever been bored - not once - not ever.

In many ways all of my running, right from those very early runs in the dark, has been therapy to me. In 2013 I ran 28 miles a day for 28 days, and every day I enjoyed five or six hours out on the road listening to my favourite prog rock anthems. It was a really therapeutic process.

Some people need to be surrounded by others all the time and they need to be able to tell those people all the time about how they feel. For me, I'm afraid, they're just Energy Vampires. They suck the lifeblood out of me. I loathe negativity... these people just don't see the big picture. When I reached my Point Zero I wasn't well - psychologically I was depressed, I was also alcohol-dependent and I was in a really awful place. In order to get out of that place I had to see the big picture. The big picture was - hold on a minute, look at all these people in your life that are enabling you to do all the bad stuff that you're doing. You've got to clean up your act and actually you have got to stick at it. If you don't, you've had it. Simple.

So, at the Stratford Half Marathon, as I came around the corner into the village where I used to live, my parents' neighbours were clapping and shouting, 'Well done! Keep going!' When really they must have been thinking, 'Oh my God, he's pulled himself together. He was circling the drain but he's cleaned himself up.' I could see all these people looking at me trying to stifle their surprise - they were genuinely shocked. They'd seen me grow up as a really nice young child and turn into somebody who was pretty unpleasant. So it was great to see all their smiling faces. My God, I felt so proud of myself!

But then there's nothing negative about running a half-marathon through the village where you used to live, is there? It was a brilliant experience and I loved it, saying to myself, 'I'm going to be under two hours today as well!' That race was my first Everest.

I used to keep a little training diary and afterwards I wrote, 'I did a half-marathon and nobody can take that away from me.' I felt like it was the beginning of a new life chapter. It was a real Zero-to-Hero moment, losing three stone in weight and transforming from the smoker-drinker-fat-guy into a half-marathon runner. And that was only between 5<sup>th</sup> January and 24<sup>th</sup> April, 1994 - that's a very short period of time. Those three months represented one of the highest points in my life so far.

Before turning my gaze to my first London Marathon in 1995, I actually ran the Telford Marathon that same year, in November 1994, thinking, 'What if I die on camera at the London Marathon and everyone sees it on BBC TV?' Running Telford would be a great trial run. It wasn't the biggest of road marathons but I gave it my best. At the halfway point I was going strong and couldn't see any other runners, so I asked one of the marshals if I was winning! Winning?! He just looked at me like my lights had gone out, like, 'What?' Of course I wasn't and when I got to 20 miles, I hit the proverbial 'wall' and had to jog-walk the last six miles, finishing it in 4 hours 4 minutes 16 seconds.

As for the winning, well in my own way yes I had... it was just one of those moments for me - 'Ker-ching! I'd only gone and bloody well done it!' When people asked me, 'What did you do at the weekend?' I simply said, 'Oh, I ran a marathon.' and they said, 'Really?' because it was quite a big deal back then, especially for the 'Me' they'd previously known.

There were only 56 days between the Telford Marathon and the London Marathon and, ironically, I was actually on the BBC TV London Marathon Highlights programme that night crossing the finish line. My arms were in the air, big smile, weighing 12 stone, well under four hours, and that was it - I was hooked. From that point onwards, I've run a marathon every week - no matter what.

# CHAPTER THREE

## A SERIES OF FIRSTS

FLY ON A WINDSHIELD - GENESIS 1974

*This is 'Real Genesis' (Banks, Collins, Gabriel, Hackett & Rutherford) at their peak in my opinion. I love the anticipation as the mood of this multi-layered music builds in true prog rock fashion right up until the drums and lead guitar kick in halfway through. The track segways into Broadway Melody of 1974 which I could have also chosen but I like the way I'm always left wanting more of everything after listening to this song and often play it over and over again on runs. The lyrics mirror my feelings about writing this book and how I feel now that I'm at the start of a whole new journey.*

These days it's not unusual for me to run three marathons on three consecutive days, often with clients I'm training for an upcoming Marathon des Sables. Sometimes it can be every day of my working week - in 2013 I clocked up 28 miles a day for 28 days ('28-in-28') for 'Stoptober', a government stop-smoking campaign. It sounds like a lot, but actually I really enjoyed it and it gave me the opportunity to be the figurehead for a cause which is very close to my heart. The way I see it, I could be sat at a desk in an office doing a really mundane job which I'd find really uninspiring and far more sapping.

Unlike my clients, I didn't start off with a running mentor. Instead, it was a copy of 'Runner's World' magazine which first caught my attention and propelled me towards running even longer distances than the standard marathon of 26 miles and 385 yards. It was the November 1994 issue that really fired my imagination. It was published whilst I was training for my first London Marathon and contained a special feature on ultra-running - the task of running beyond a marathon. Inside there was a picture of an American lady called Ann Trason and there was a feature on her running the Western States Endurance Race in America. It was that image that rocked my world. I saw that photograph of her running up the Rocky Mountains and I just thought, 'That's what I want to do!'

Of course, I didn't have a clue how I'd make that dream a reality. I just saw a photo of her and thought, 'Gosh, she looks great!' It just looked incredible, brilliant. It was like, 'I want some of that.' What she was doing was totally surreal to me, it was different to anything I'd ever seen before, it was totally 'far out' and way beyond any running concept I had ever come across. What she was doing was also completely off my scale. But I just sat there looking at that amazing amount of freedom she was experiencing and thought, 'Wow!'

There was also an article on Alberto Salazar who'd won the prestigious 56 mile Comrades Marathon in South Africa. I just saw these people and thought, 'That's it. That's my destiny.' I felt inspired to go and grab some of what they were having. I knew that it was possible if I trained really hard - having run my first marathon I'd acquired a taste for distance and knew I could go a lot further.

From that day forwards I was hooked - I was fascinated by the concept of ultra-running and the next logical step for me was to really start upping my mileage. Not that I'd been taking running lightly up until this point - by now I was already testing myself, I'd tried a week running 10 miles a day every day - it was brilliant! I did them all in about 80 minutes. I just went and ran them. It was great. It does sound bizarre now, and I'm not being glib, it was just what I really, really wanted to do. It was the sense of freedom that it gave me. I was thinking, 'Well, I wonder how many other people are running 10 miles a day. I wonder - is anybody else doing what I'm doing?'

My new training regime became nine miles in the morning and nine miles in the evening, four days a week. Then I'd run 20 miles on a Saturday and 20 miles on a Sunday. That's as technical as it got. I know suddenly running all those miles sounds like I was in self-destruction mode, but I wasn't. It was a positive mental and physical building process. Naturally I had some initial aches and pains, like lots of runners do when they start off, but my body adjusted very quickly to the new regime. I guess it's comparable to tasting beer or cigarettes for the first time - they don't taste brilliant but you persevere.

Cigarettes and alcohol are actually horrible when you start - the first time you try to smoke you cough your guts up; the first time you try lager you just go, 'Ah yuk that's awful.' But then you sort of get a taste for it, don't you? And you start seeing the benefits of it. When you start drinking it lowers your inhibitions, you go out to pubs, you meet girls, you make friends, and it feels like a very sociable thing to do. Maybe running was my new addiction?

In no time I was on a roll - 3 miles, 5 miles, 10 miles, 20 miles a day... I was conquering Everest on a daily basis. And when you are doing that you don't give a second thought to toxins like cigarettes and alcohol - the running buzz was infinitely better! They became irrelevant very quickly - a thing of the past never to re-embrace - they became easy to extinguish from my everyday life. So much so that I've never felt the lure to go back to either and rely on them once again.

My days now began at 5:30am - I was totally driven to get the miles under my belt. My wife didn't mind, or actually really say anything about it at the time. I think she was just relieved that I was getting up and going to do something productive rather than waking up groggy from the night before. Plus it didn't have any impact on our family life - I'd be back in just over an hour as I'd gotten faster and faster at covering that nine mile distance. Some days I'd really go for it and get it done quickly, but by in large my goal at the time was to run slower in the morning and to step it up in the evening.

This training regime made me feel euphoric - every day was like Christmas! I didn't worry about all the running I was doing, or question the distances I was covering, because I figured that my body could handle whatever I threw at it. After all, if I could knock back 10 pints of Stella and smoke 40 cigarettes a day and still function, my body must be pretty bombproof! With a fresh head and time to myself, all that running enabled me to put some order back into my life - to get a new perspective on things. Everything in my life had gotten so jumbled. I felt like I was cleaning myself from the inside out - it was a complete life-laundry.

Up until the end of 1994 I was in my own little world - I hadn't thought I was good enough to join a running club. I was a fat drinker-smoker who used running as therapy to sort his shit out and change from person 'A' to person 'B'. Once I'd run my first marathon, however, I started to gain more confidence in my ability and began to perceive myself as an Athlete. So after a while I thought it would be great to meet some like-minded people, and with my newfound intrigue of ultra-running I knew that joining a club would help me to progress my training more quickly. So eventually I joined the Stratford-upon-Avon Athletic Club.

Disappointingly, when I finally decided to go along to the running club to join, I found out that there wasn't really anyone there like me. They were people who were busy, wanting to run shorter distances and races than I did - 5k/10k races, cross-country, or maybe a triathlon. Only a few of its members ran marathons - they were a Big Deal - a Major Commitment. There didn't seem to be anyone there who wanted to just go and, well, run, all day. That's all I wanted to do. My personal life wasn't great and my working life was going through a transition - running was a huge ray of sunshine for me.

Then one night I was introduced to an old guy called John Martin at the Club - he was in his late sixties and came from Redcar, near Middlesbrough. He was somebody that got into running in his fifties and followed the coaching ideals of Arthur Lydiard - a highly renowned coach in New Zealand in the 1950's. He'd trained some of New Zealand's Olympic Gold-Medal Winning athletes. John had been using a technique whereby you ran up to 200 miles a week and then, as race day approached, you'd taper down for four weeks and concentrate on speed work.

John and I hit it off immediately because both of us liked running 20 miles a day at the weekend. He was retired, but he was actually quite spritely for his age. Together we'd go and run 20 miles in around four and a half hours, which seemed to take forever at the time. So I'd do all these nine milers during the week, have a day off, and then go and run 20 miles with John on a Saturday and 20 miles again with him on a Sunday. And during the time that we ran together he would tell me all about his own running and all about the coaching ideals of Arthur Lydiard. He's the guy that taught me how to run.

When my first London Marathon came around on 2nd April, 1995, I knew I was ready. At the time all you had to do was fill in your entry form, send it off with a cheque and you were in - no waiting list like there is today - HOORAH! So come race day, there I am! I'm running around the Cutty Sark, over Tower Bridge, over the famous cobbles, through all these places that David Coleman had been commentating about on TV for years and years and years. And there I was - I was actually doing the race myself.

As I reached the final stages and ran around the corner at the top of Buckingham Palace, then down The Mall, I'm not kidding, it was a spectacular place to be. I think everybody should do it once in their life. It would be an amazing experience in and of itself, but the fact that you're just about to complete the London Marathon is the tastiest ever icing on the cake. There was also the kudos - in those days folk were impressed when you said you'd done the London Marathon as not many people had run it. It's not quite the same these days.

Still, my first London experience was an overwhelming success - all that training with John had paid off - I jogged round in 3 hours 54 minutes. I really did just jog round effortlessly that day. Afterwards I got in the car, I drove home and I mowed the lawn. I was lucky - it normally takes years for the human body to build up that kind of endurance. Your heart is a muscle and must grow like any other muscle to meet your increased need for oxygen, particularly if you are running for prolonged periods of time. Your legs also have to adapt to the constant strain of running. You usually have to go through periods of injury and rehabilitation. Your body has to learn. There are so many things that go against you when you start running, especially when you step up to doing high mileage training. But I was just physically there very quickly. It was like, 'Bang! I've got it!'

Nonetheless, my running was far from perfect at this stage - I lacked experience, knowledge and some goals to strive for. When you start running you're on a journey from 'A' (your starting point) to 'B' (your end goal) with 'T' (time) in the middle. My problem was that I didn't really have a goal - I didn't know what my 'B' was. I knew where I had started, my 'A', but I was just using running as therapy with no specific goals in mind - I needed some direction as I didn't know how long 'T' was. Nowadays, if I was training you to do the London Marathon in April for example, your 'A' is the day we start training, your 'B' is your race day in April and I know what 'T' is, because I could say, 'Okay, you've got 84 days until the London Marathon at this moment in time and we can work out a training schedule to get you round.' Without the same parameters all I was doing was using running as a salvation.

Once I had run the London Marathon, I couldn't stop. Within a month I did another one - the Stratford Marathon. A few weeks after that, Hereford, and very quickly I was doing one a week just to get that feeling of coming down the last 385 yards of the marathon, because it's so amazing. That feeling of accomplishment! Of positivity! It was my Christmas. It was just the best Christmas present ever, every time I ran down that line. As a consequence my life got into a rhythm... I discovered the parameters... I'd run a marathon on the Sunday, recover on the Monday, go back to running on the Tuesday, Wednesday, Thursday and by Friday I was looking forward to the next marathon.

It was during this time that I met Big Dave Carter. Now if you've met Big Dave, you'll understand why he's called Big Dave. He's just a giant guy - 20+ stone and well over six feet tall, and he'd run more marathons than me at the time. I had started bumping into the same like-minded people on the marathon running circuit, so I'd do a marathon and see Big Dave at the start line. I'd just sort of say, 'Oh hi, how are you doing?' as he was always there, at the same races as me.

Dave was a kindred spirit. It was like having a drinking buddy, only he was a marathon junkie running buddy. I'd still go everywhere with John. I'd take him with me because he lived in Stratford-upon-Avon, but I'd meet up with Dave once I was there, and a lot of the time I ended up running with him.

I was happy just clocking up the marathons. I was only competitive a couple of times a year - in April (the London Marathon) and September (the Robin Hood Marathon, unsurprisingly in Nottingham). London because it was London and it's the one that everyone in the UK is aware of. For example, when I set a Guinness World Record for running on a treadmill later on in 1998, covering 101.36 miles in a day, somebody said to me afterwards, 'Yeah, but have you done the London Marathon…?' The Robin Hood because I had a really good run there the first year I entered (1995) - 3 hours 30 minutes and the course certainly wasn't flat. In fact I've had a good run at Robin Hood ever since. At the time of writing I've done both the London and Robin Hood Marathons over 10 times each and they are races which hold a very special place in my heart.

The brilliant thing about running with Dave was that together we got to take advantage of the fact that I had a company car with a petrol account. We'd regularly drive into Europe and run two marathons over the course of a weekend. We'd get on the ferry to France, drive down to the Médoc Marathon near Bordeaux - ironically a wine marathon where they give out wine at the checkpoints as well as water. The next day we'd do another in Cahors then drive back to the UK in time to return to work on the Monday morning.

When I wasn't running marathons I continued running 20 milers with John, still soaking up his running know-how. My body was feeling the positive effects of living by John's long-distance rules - in other words, I did lots and lots of long slow distance - he called it LSD running.

To this day I have continued to do an enormous amount of LSD. It's made my heart bigger - my heart is now 1.6 times the size it would have been without doing all that endurance. In fact, whilst the average male heart rate is 72 beats per minute (bpm), mine has been as low as 37bpm. That said, given the amount of running I do, my average heart rate on a lot of days is between 100 and 140 bpm. It's said that there are 2.5 billion heartbeats in a lifetime so I do wonder if I'm using them up at a quicker rate than I should.

Maybe I am, but actually I see it another way - I'm now 14 years older than my Doctor Brother predicted if I didn't change my lifestyle. So in a way I'm in a win-win situation. Every day is a bonus. That's probably why, these days, I live mostly in the here and now - much like how you think whilst you're running, you're just putting one foot in front of the other, and that's all you're focusing on.

As well as learning about LSD whilst we ran long loops around Stratford-upon-Avon John would tell me about his slant on life, how he saw things. We ran hundreds of miles together, actually, and I learnt so much invaluable information. I learnt a lot about what shoes to wear, what socks to wear, how to prepare for races. He had an amazing trainer collection! They were all really, really good quality shoes but because of the mileage that he was running, he literally wore them out in two to three weeks!

It was the same for me - we were putting in so many miles they needed constant replacement. Last year I thought I'd see what happened if I tried to run the 28-in-28 in one pair of trainers. I wore a pair of Brooks trainers - my all-time favourite brand - and they lasted 20 days, or 560 miles. They had moulded to my feet perfectly but eventually lost all of their spring. When I replaced them with a new pair it took me two days to 'break them in' and make them as comfortable as the ones I'd worn out.

John also taught me practical lessons about running which were invaluable when I ran from London to Lisbon in Portugal. For example, I ran on the left hand side of the road, into the oncoming traffic, whilst wearing a different type of shoe on each foot to allow for the camber of the road. It worked a treat - each shoe was a different height as each ankle needed different support, exacerbated by the fact that my left leg is slightly longer than my right.

As my mileage has increased over the years, I have never forgotten the crucial lessons that John imparted to me. I still wear good running shoes at all times. I still have a day off if I feel tired. I still clock up the miles doing the long slow distance he preached about. All those lessons from him are now my basic running vocabulary. It's common sense - it's now 'Coleman Sense'... See what I did there?

Whilst John definitely had by the far the biggest impact on my running career, my inspiration for the sport has also been drawn from role models outside the world of running. People like George Best, Alex Higgins and Paul Gascoigne - people who have been utterly gifted and blown it! They're guys who had a huge natural gift in their own specific fields of sport and basically self-destructed. It's catastrophic that they didn't fulfil their potential - I didn't want to be one of them. I wanted to do the best that I possibly could with my running. The more I ran, the more I wanted to be that person on the cover of Runner's World.

So later in life, when I embarked upon my career as a personal trainer and performance coach, I was only interested in being 'The Best'. I didn't want to be somebody who just worked at a gym, cleaned machines and took the odd bland training session. I wanted to be known for being 'The Best Coach' there was. Initially, the drive and passion I'd developed for running and excelling did have its drawbacks as far as my coaching was concerned - I found it hard to relate to clients complaining about their inability to run relatively short distances and couldn't understand why they couldn't be enthused by running like I was.

Indeed, I've heard some terrible excuses in my time and often get frustrated by social media, for example where somebody says they dropped out of a race and they receive comments such as, 'Well, that was a really good thing, because you don't want to cause yourself any long term injury.' Or, 'Well done anyway. Good effort you should be proud you got that far.' I can't think of any long term injury that's come from jogging another however many miles. It's just an excuse not to do something.

So what I've done in recent years is separate the two things completely: there's My running, and then there's My Clients' running. There's nothing worse than proudly telling your coach, 'I've done my five miles this morning,' only to be trumped by, 'Well done - I did 15.' So I tell my clients, 'That's great! Tell me what happened! Do you feel you need to speed up? Do you need to lose some weight?' With them I'm trying to encourage them to get the best out of themselves, it's not about me when I'm with them.

The interesting thing is that lots of my clients are far better runners than I am, they just don't apply themselves in the same way. I'm certainly not the most gifted runner that has ever lived. I've just wanted things more than anyone else. This has enabled me to achieve some extraordinary things with a relatively ordinary body - Guinness World Records, back-to-back marathons, ultras and so on. What I've been able to do is use my attributes to their maximum capacity. I've had numerous fitness tests over the years by those studying the effects of long-distance on the body and vice versa. From these tests, I've learnt that the one advantage I *do* have on my side is a very high haematocrit level - that's the quantity of red blood cells that I have travelling around my body. It's a hereditary trait which basically means that my oxygen delivery is really good and enables me to work aerobically for a long time.

I'm also very, very determined. I think my addiction-riddled past helps me to continue at moments when other people might falter. Maybe my past has hardened me up. Have you ever got up for work after a really heavy night the night before when you really don't want to? At one period in my life that was my everyday reality. But when it comes to running, I've been The Best In The World - I've been The Best In The World nine times - I've got the Guinness World Record Certificates hanging on my wall to prove it and it's funny how that came about…

Around about the same time I met Big Dave Carter - after running the London Marathon followed by 11 marathons in 11 weeks - I thought, 'Gosh that must be a record.' It was a Monday morning and the idea of being a record breaker filled my thoughts. I was working opposite a WHSmith at the time so I nipped straight over the road and bought the 1998 Guinness Book of Records to see what the world records were for marathon-running. The men's world record was 2:06:50 at the time... so I thought, 'Oh I don't think I'll challenge that one!' Even the running backwards one looked a bit quick! There wasn't really anything in there that I could see where I could shine as far as the standard marathon distance was concerned.

There was, however, an American lady who had run 93 miles on a treadmill in 24 hours who was also listed as a Guinness World Record holder. I thought, '93 miles? I reckon I could do that, in fact I reckon I could set a number of treadmill records to stand alongside those recorded for ultra-distances around the track.' In the world of ultra-running, there were records for distances covered in 12 hours, 24 hours, 48 hours and even a week. So I contacted Guinness and said to them, 'Look, I want to go and beat the 24 hour treadmill record but I also want to set ones for 12 hours, 50 miles, 100km and 100 miles as well and they went, 'Yeah, that's great. We love it.' I'd found a great opportunity to make my mark on the World.

So on 17-18th October, 1998 at Stratford-upon-Avon Leisure Centre, I set the Guinness World Record for 'The Furthest Distance Covered on a Treadmill in 24 Hours' - I ran 101.36 miles. Whilst I was running for 24 hours, I also set records for the furthest distance in 12 hours as well as the quickest 50 miles, 100km and 100 miles. After that, I thought, 'Well if I can run on it for one day, maybe I could run on it for two.' So next I set the 48 Hour World Record, and then eventually in 2001, I went on to set the Week World Record where I ran as far as I could in seven days. To polish that one off, I ran the London Marathon as a warm down on the eighth day. I was even invited to complete the last four days of my weeklong treadmill record at the London Marathon Exhibition...

So there I was, running on a treadmill in the middle of the London Arena, setting a World Record in front of tens of thousands of runners who had come to register for the London Marathon. Sky TV and the BBC TV News were there filming, even David Bedford - the Race Director of the London Marathon - was interested in what I was doing. He remarked that I was, 'Totally bonkers!' The whole experience was one of the real high points of my running career.

That was when the London Marathon was far less popular than it is today. I often wonder how much more publicity that stunt would attract these days but I always come to the same conclusion - probably no more than it did back then. In 2001 it was new, I was a maverick, it was unfathomable and people just didn't get it. Nowadays, ultra-marathons are far more mainstream and participation of the general population in leisure activities has risen dramatically. So rather than paying for a season ticket for their football team, these days people invest in training for a life challenge such as a triathlon, a marathon or an ultra.

Running is a relatively cheap leisure activity - you buy some trainers you go for a run - all you really need is a decent pair of trainers. However, with the advent of the Internet, what *is* expensive is the (now vast) array of enticing races you can enter at the drop of some credit card details. The Internet has just completely expanded people's running horizons. Photography is such a powerful tool. You see all these incredible images of people enjoying out-of-this-world experiences - running in extraordinary landscapes, in extraordinary climates and, subconsciously, you cut out their heads from these photos and replace them with your own. It's the online version of my first glance at that picture of Ann Trason in Runner's World running the Western States Endurance Race. In reality, I wanted a picture of me doing that same race. I could actually picture myself doing it. Do I think people now cut my head off and put their own head onto my body? Yes I do - as I write this book I've run 976 marathons and that's something that just blows people away. That's quite an ego boost! In a way that means I am to others what Ann Trason was to me!

That's partly what makes me tick, part of my psyche. I want to impress and to please my peer groups. I love the 'Wow!' factor. Like everyone, there are certainly things about me that I'm not so proud of. I'd be the first to admit I've had my fair share of failings but I don't really want to go and stand in front of people and say, 'By the way, I've been married three times.' My running records, however, they're real accomplishments, aren't they? They're the things that I like to announce.

But even when I started making a name for myself in the running world, I was still running with Big Dave no matter what else I had going on. He was my main ally at this point, partly because I really looked up to him and partly because he's such fun to be around. He'd been Daily Mirror Slimmer of the Year in his past - he'd got down to about 16 stone when he had actually looked positively anorexic. Yes, he's a huge guy, with a huge personality. He'd still run some good times - 3:25 or so at London one year. We had so much in common - like me he'd been unhappy, been divorced and found his working life uninspiring. He also used running as his release. He just got it and I thought, 'He's just like me.' We still call each other 'My Bestest Marathon Running Buddy in the Whole World Ever.'

There were lots of other people out there running marathons every weekend but they weren't like him. They didn't have the same fun outlook on life that Dave had. Dave liked the same music and wanted to go to the same places as me. So we just went there and did it. It was great. I probably ran over 100 marathons with him all over the world. We ran in Chicago, Stockholm, Helsinki, Monaco, everywhere. We did them in fancy dress and had amazing tales to tell afterwards. When you get to share those kinds of adventures with somebody else, you get to say, 'Remember that whatever marathon - it was the wettest, hottest, hardest! Oh, remember that drive, ferry or flight? It was hellish!' You start building up history with somebody. He was my enabler when I decided to start racking up the marathons, when I started to get carried away with the numbers, when I started to play the numbers game - how many marathons had I done compared to everyone else...?

My proud parents actually came to see my 100th marathon. It was in July 1998 in Rottingdean, Sussex. It was an incredibly wet and awfully muddy Sunday. The only thing I can tell you about the whole thing is that I ran round with Dave, and he did a complete nosedive into this huge muddy puddle. Two ladies pulled him out and he was just brown from head to toe! I laughed so much! It was just absolutely side-splitting the way he'd gone down. It was almost like he'd done it as a 100th marathon celebration present.

He got his own back though as on another occasion we were running an off-road race in Wales across this massive field and for some bizarre reason there was a hosepipe running across the middle of it. Of course the inevitable happened and I somehow managed to trip over it flying headlong into a load of cow pats. And of course he split his sides. It was great banter, like being back at my old grammar school. We would constantly be ribbing each other. And that was part of the fun of all this running. We were like a Morecambe & Wise comedy duo.

Admittedly, there were people at these races who didn't think we took them very seriously at times, the kind who spent hours analysing all their results in the deepest, darkest detail. We just weren't like that. That's not to say I disregard or have a problem with people who obsess over the minutiae of their race performances - I just have to respect that that's part of the satisfaction they get from running. I also find it hard to relate to people I meet at races who are obsessed with just getting to the finish line, hell for leather, head down. They miss so much by not allowing themselves to lap up the ever changing environment around them. I always look around and try to take in the world when I run.

In fact, the more marathons Dave and I ran, the more we noticed that there were definitely different runner 'types', a sort of running hierarchy. You tended to be split by your marathon times. So if you were a sub-3 hour guy, you were one type of person. Then there were the 3 to 3.5 hour guys, then 3.5 to 4 hour guys, and then you were an 'over 4'. And in fact I once said to myself, 'If I ever run over four hours I'll pack up.' I couldn't believe that anyone would need to take more than four hours to run a marathon. I could run a 3.5 hour marathon every weekend; I'd just do them at that pace all the time but then I was incredibly fit and in my early thirties at the time.

Now though, my approach is very different, especially when it comes to doing events like the 28-in-28. I ran each of them in 5.5 hours because I've changed from being a keen club runner-type athlete to becoming this mega-day ultra-marathoner that can do back-to-back marathons for weeks. In fact, one of the goals that remains on my bucket list is to run a marathon every day for a year. It's there in big, bold, flashing letters. I know I could definitely do it - I'm a diesel engine these days - I'm all about efficiency! But even for someone who places such importance on their leisure time, life does impose some limitations.

The men and women who do marathons in just over two hours - they're just incredible athletes, aren't they? Anybody that can run under 2.5 hours for a marathon is a truly great athlete and a totally different runner to me. They're built in a completely different way. I'm not built like a marathon runner. My body's got a different type of muscle structure to it. Those men and women are very, very lean, mean, fighting machines. They probably weigh less than 63kg. I don't. I weigh 80kg. I'm six feet tall and my BMI's 24, so I don't have a runner's build.

I'm more of a tennis player build, really. I once ran 3:24:21, and that's my marathon PB. That's the fastest I could go. It's the fastest my ability could take me. In fact, most people can run a marathon in under four hours in my opinion. Two hour marathon success though comes down to an in-built natural ability. If I was tiny, I'd be a Marathon World Record Beater with my mind-set, I know it.

But Dave and I - we just ran marathons for fun. I'm sure we rubbed a few folk up the wrong way but I'm a bit of a marmite character - you either like me or you don't. I'm very much somebody that you either get or you don't get. Also by doing all this running, I've put myself into a position where some people are jealous of what I've achieved and others are critical of my accomplishments. But you can't please everyone can you?

Life was one long marathon road trip. We were clocking up marathons at an incredible rate - it only took me 3 years and 322 days to clock up that 100th marathon and only 419 days for the next hundred. Much of that focus came down to the fact that I have always been a 'Big Picture' person - every marathon I do, everything I accomplish, is all part of a bigger picture - running 1,000 marathons was (and still is) mine. There are certain sacrifices that you have to make along the way and I have, and will continue to make, those sacrifices.

So if I decided that I was going to do a mega-day challenge whilst holding down a job I'd just say, 'I need six weeks off,' and if they said, 'Well you can't have six weeks off!' then I'd say, 'Well, cheerio, I'll go and get another job.' That is exactly what happened on one such occasion. Or if I just needed time off and their reply was, 'Well, we're not going to pay you,' my response would be, 'Okay, that's fine,' because I was more interested in actually going and doing this extraordinary thing. I think a lot of people live to work. I work to live.

In those early years I didn't meet any criticism from anyone, maybe because not a lot of people really knew what I was doing.

Actually, I didn't really know what I was doing either but I just kept planning and ticking off the next Everest.

My journey into ultras had started with the 'Grantham Canal Race' from Nottingham to Grantham - it was 33 miles and 1,660 yards long. I ran it like a marathon, completing it in 5 hours 2 minutes, which was a good time on the grassy towpath. I loved it. It took place on the August Bank Holiday 1995 - only my tenth ever race. On that day there was another runner doing the race from my running club so I thought I'd better try and beat him. We ran side by side for 20 miles then I pushed on and burned him off. I thought, 'I can't let him beat me.' Did he want to beat me? Of course he did but I wanted the folk in my club to see that I was a better runner than he was. I also wanted to see if I could run hard all the way to the finish, and I could...

... And herein, for me, lies the problem with people running ultras. Admittedly, it's far more relaxed at the back of the pack in a marathon, but what happens with ultra-marathon running is that people believe they can take even longer - that they can run/walk/crawl at a very slow pace - because of the added distance. ANY pace is considered acceptable - it's covering the distance and reaching the finish line that counts. It's wrong really, as there's more enjoyment in running fast and setting PB's in my opinion - at the Grantham Canal Race I ran just under nine minute miles all the way. It felt great.

And of course when you do that, you go, 'Well I've done 33 miles, maybe I can do a 50-miler. Maybe I can do an 80-miler. Maybe I can do 100, or even further.' So I started looking for bigger races as I hadn't yet found a limit to my endurance.

'London to Brighton' ticked all the boxes. It was a 55-mile race on the road from Big Ben to Brighton's Sea Front Marina which I ran three times. I did it in 9:24, 9:16 and finally 8:55 - my quickest. It was definitely far more enjoyable that year as I smashed the nine hour barrier and my course PB too, just a week after clocking up a 3:32 at the Robin Hood Marathon.

I was now running at my full potential. It was a great week of running for me. A great seven days of running in my life. I'd run in the UK's premier long distance race finishing quite high up in the field. I was an ex-drinker/smoker running with the best runners in the UK. It felt like I'd arrived.

I view your average runner's body like a classic Porsche car that is only taken to the track occasionally - it's only taken out for a proper spin a few weekends a year. In contrast, I tend to compare myself to the latest Audi Sport that races around the track for 24 hours at Le Mans. The Porsche wouldn't go the distance if you took it to Le Mans - it's not really been tested or pushed to its limits. I'm prepared for the demands of running for hours and hours. Over my 22 years of running, I've come to understand my body telemetry and know exactly what makes me tick. I understand all the feedback.

Obviously, there is an enormous sense of achievement you get from running ultra-marathons. For me, this feeling of achievement is directly proportional to the distance I have accomplished. That said, what I also love about ultra-running is that you get to the stage where it becomes a spiritual thing to do.

So if you're on the road for days and days, like I was in 2004 when I was running from London to Lisbon in Portugal, you begin to run at a sort of higher state of awareness. I could feel every stone under my feet. It's like a pianist's touch - you become totally tuned in to your body. You could call it a Zen State, you can call it whatever you like, but for me it's just part of the joy of running and an amazing natural feeling. I was on the road for the duration of the adventure and must have been passed by a million cars or more - I didn't have any near misses with any of them, I didn't even notice them, I felt touched by a higher power and believed that God was looking out for me.

There were days when I just stopped and looked at my surroundings. I met God and Heaven all in one place in Spain - I actually stopped and thought, 'This place looks idyllic, and if

Heaven's going to exist for me I want it to look like this.' So I just stopped, sat down, and took in my surroundings. I sat there for about 20 minutes. I took a photo of that moment to remind me what it's going to look like. I've even named it 'Heaven'.

I was in the middle of this rolling countryside in Spain. There were fields of corn, like the ones that Russell Crowe's wife puts her hands through in the film 'Gladiator'. The corn was gently blowing from side to side, there was this little village with its Church tower and the sun was shining - it just looked fabulous. And I thought, 'Gosh I've found it. Isn't this amazing? How can it all be here by chance, what a dull idea that would be - so maybe there is creation and it was created by somebody.' Maybe I did feel like there was an arm around my shoulder supporting me for all those weeks on the road.

It also happened in 2013 when I was doing the 28-in-28. I had been listening to my prog rock which was great, but after 25 days of the same playlist I was in need of a change. I decided to put on some 'Live' albums that I'd enjoyed listening to in my youth. So, armed with some Steve Hillage from 1978, I was running along and the world became perfectly clear. It was like everything just slotted into place. I was ticking along with a heart-rate of just under 100bpm at a really easy pace, the sun was shining and I just thought, 'Do you know what? The world is a brilliant place!' I couldn't feel any exertion, and everything went calm. It was just an amazing feeling. I'm sure no-one has ever had that feeling on the way into Swindon, but I did.

During my London to Lisbon adventure I covered 30 miles a day for 43 days without an injury. I got to the end in one piece. It was a real journey and an amazing life experience. Looking back I think, 'Oh my God!' It's one of the best things I've ever done. In over 1,275 miles I'd emptied my head. I managed to get rid of all of the baggage in my mind - all that pent up stuff from the past - to clear out my thoughts, to think about who I really was, what I wanted to do with my life, all of those things.

People get caught up in the pedantries of everyday life... they get road rage in cars but it's just futile isn't it? Others get caught up in celebrity culture - I hate all that stuff. There are many better things to do in life - I've found out about my spiritual self through running. The journeys that I've had to do to get to that place. Some people go on retreats but for me, running through life's various chapters has given me a better grasp of who I am.

To get to that point in my running I've had to work hard, it's about investment. I had to invest in bucket loads of sweat. Just like you don't become a cross-channel swimmer overnight - first you have to swim a few lengths of the pool, then you have to get really good in the pool, then you have to swim in the sea. You discover how hard it is to swim in the sea but the more you sea-swim, the better it gets and if you're trying to swim the channel, well you have to be at the peak of your lifetime fitness to achieve your goal.

# CHAPTER FOUR

## GOING ULTRA

UNINVITED - FREEMASONS (FEATURING BAILEY TZUKE) 2007

*The Freemasons' Production Team of Russell Small and James Wiltshire injected the X-Factor into this brilliant rework of Alanis Morissette's rather dark original, making it a stand out track for me. This track was played on a loop at Fitness First in Derby, where I worked out of for three years, so it must have been drilled deep down into my sub-consciousness. For me, there's a fantastic feel-good factor that accompanies this song because I loved that time in my life where I was learning and starting over professionally.*

When I first became interested in racing, there was a publication that all long-distance runners relied on for race information - we didn't have the Internet, you see. It came from 'The Road Runners Club' and listed every marathon in the UK.

It's fascinating, actually, to think how times have changed. Back in the early eighties there were over 140 marathons in the UK - there was one in every city or large town - it was the real boom of marathon running. By the mid-nineties, that boom had ended with only around a quarter of those races still running. Thankfully, there seems to have been a steady revival of marathons since then and there is currently a superb choice of races to take part in all over the UK.

Anyway, this book became a daily read for me - I was clocking up races like they were going out of fashion - and I slavered over its contents as if they were runners' porn! That's how I discovered the Grantham Canal Run which was still quite a new event in 1995. I was living in Stratford-upon-Avon at the time and my parents kindly agreed to take me to the race. They were my moral support, plus I thought it wouldn't be sensible to drive myself all the way back to Stratford-upon-Avon after my first Ultra. There was also the added complication that the course was point-to-point, i.e. it started in one place and finished in another - having a support crew at these sorts of races is always a bonus.

Nonetheless, it was the moral support I was really after - having them there cheering me on at the finish line felt really good. And they made a day of it too - after dropping me at the start they did a few hours of shopping in Grantham. But they were there to see me at the end and it felt like they were proud of me, how far I'd come, how I'd changed. I don't remember them ever communicating these thoughts explicitly - I knew they didn't want me to revert back to my old ways and I think they didn't want to jinx anything by saying something that might upset me and send me spiralling backwards.

But then they'd always been there for me when I needed their support as a child. In fact, even when I speak to my parents now they still think of me as their little lad. When I was 13, four decades ago now, I got my cricketing scholarship with Warwickshire County Cricket Club. Every week, I'd have to finish school 10 minutes early so that we could drive all the way to Birmingham for the practice nets. It was quite a drive to Edgbaston and I had to get there for 5:00pm on the dot. So every Tuesday night, my poor Dad would be driving like a Formula 1 racing driver all the way to Birmingham, some 25 miles from Stratford-upon-Avon, to get me to Edgbaston in time to spend two hours in the nets. That was an enormous commitment from them.

By the time I reached 18, I was playing cricket four times a week… but then I went to art school and discovered beer, cigarettes and girls. The cricket, funnily enough, was relegated - I had new distractions. My thought process at the time was, 'You're spending all day playing cricket on a Saturday and on a Sunday, and you're not getting girlfriends or going to parties like your mates are.' So the cricket became more of a hindrance at the time even though later, of course, I wished I had pursued it further. But that's life, isn't it? Deep down, maybe I knew I wasn't good enough to be The Best.

Anyway, back to my 1995 Grantham Canal Run experience… I found out at the start of the race that there had been a 36 miler the previous day in Scotland - 'The Two Bridges' - which was marginally longer than the 33.94 mile Grantham race. To my astonishment, there were runners setting off with me who'd already completed the one in Scotland the day before - they'd driven through the night to get to Grantham just so they could do a double ultra.

At the start, the race organiser gathered everyone together for a race briefing, and during this briefing he actually pointed these people out. Everybody clapped and cheered in amazement and I thought, 'That's cool,' and decided, 'I must do that in the future.' For me, that was something to aspire to.

When I got to the finish in Grantham I was pretty tired. I sat down and remember having a big blanket wrapped around me to keep me warm - it had been a tough day. My Mum, Dad and I all staggered back to the car. It had been a real test of both my physical and mental endurance. Physically, I had given it everything I had for a whole eight miles further than I had ever run before. Mentally, I hadn't known if my legs were going to fall off at 30 miles as I'd never run that far before, so I just ran along its grass tow path, along this disused canal, hoping beyond all hope for nearly 34 miles that I would reach the finish intact - now that was really exhausting. The course wasn't the most interesting either - there was no water in the canal, just weed. But I found the lack of distractions didn't really matter - I was thoroughly enjoying stepping up to the next level.

Funnily enough, although I've now been running for over 22 years, my marathon times haven't changed a great deal since then. My PB is 3:24:21 which I ran in 1996 whereas in 2013, I ran a 3:37 at Abingdon. But running an ultra-marathon was totally different to running a marathon - I had moved up to the next level in the running hierarchy pyramid: at the bottom you've got your 5 and 10k's, next you've got your half-marathons, marathons and ultras, then you've got multi-day races and finally, above them all, you have your running feats such as your Guinness World Records. It's a massive pyramid to climb, but you can work your way up through each stage, or 'level of apprenticeship' as I like to call it, pretty quickly if you want it badly enough.

So rather than just being one of the ants at the bottom, I decided, 'I want to be at the top of the pyramid, because I want to be The Best.'

As I started working my way up the pyramid I found that the further you run, the more your psychological strength comes into play. Your mind can play games with you and it's all about how you control it and stay positive. When I ran from London to Lisbon, for instance, I just emptied my brain - I thought about every single thing I could possibly think of. I'd spend miles playing mind games - my favourite was the Alphabet Game. I loved music so I'd be thinking, 'ABC, Black Sabbath, Cream, Depeche Mode,' and so on through the alphabet, thinking of as many groups as I could as many times through the alphabet as possible. Then I might go through and think of songs. Then I might think of all the people who were in my class at school and then I'd think about all the girlfriends I'd ever had and rank them in height, attractiveness and chest size. You play all these mental games while you're running along because your mind goes to a whole new level of consciousness.

I've been coaching for over eight years now, and during that time I've met a lot of other people who are just like the old me - it really helps me to identify their different personality traits. In fact, coaching has actually been therapeutic for me as well as for my clients - working through their issues and problems has helped me to come to terms with more of mine. So, whereas before I would only tell you about all the things I was good at: 'Yeah, yeah, I'm in the print game, I'm with the best printing company and we offer the best prices, and we're fantastic and blah, blah, blah, blah,' now I can actually say, 'Do you know what, I'm really good at this but for goodness sake don't ask me to do that because actually, I'm just not very good at it.'

My days are now super-busy and everything runs like clockwork. Everything in my life is compartmentalised and there are certain things - like planning for the long term future - that I find difficult. Does that sound selfish? Possibly, but then I think that some of the most selfish people I've ever met are ultra-runners and these are the people I connect with the best. I guess spending your free time doing what you love doing is selfish, but the flip side is that an inherent part of being a successful ultra-runner is having the drive and commitment to dedicate a significant amount of time to your training. So if you are considering embarking upon a career in ultra-running, my advice to you would be to find a partner who also enjoys and/ or participates in the sport - then you can indulge in selfishness together!

In a relatively short space of time, running became a very important and very large part of my life. Yes - I did exclude other things in life, and lots of other things suffered because of their exclusion from my thoughts. I'm sure my children suffered because I was off on huge running expeditions. My relationships suffered too - I understood that but by this point my running had become a defining feature, an integral part, of who I was. It was my identity - my 'raison d'être'.

My thought process has always been, 'If I stopped now, there's a possibility that I would regress back into the Old Rory.' Not that I can actually remember how it felt to be Old Rory - it's such a long time ago. Lots of people ask me, 'If you just took one sip of alcohol, would you become an alcoholic again?' No, I don't think so but I don't want to break my 8,000+ day record of being dry - that's really important to me because, like the lady I'm training who is a couple of months into her abstinence, I'm only one drink away from shattering my dream. So it doesn't matter that she's 60 days and I'm 8,000+ days into it really as we're actually in the same boat - just one drink away from failure and, as you are probably beginning to realise, that's not an option for me.

Why test out the theory? Why risk it? Even though I don't honestly believe one drink would start me off down a slippery slope - why do it? Why break something so precious? Why smash up my 8,000 piece ever expanding jigsaw?

When I ran my first ultra I breathed it all in - the race, the atmosphere, the scenery, that disused canal. I was interested in all the bridges and the locks and the history of the canal, and the race. Other people might just go to it and say, 'Well, all I'm interested in is that I run it in five hours. I don't give a damn about how big the locks are or how many litres of water are in them.' It all seemed part of it to me, especially limbo dancing under some of the lower bridges later on in the race.

I went on to run the Grand Union Canal Race which uses the towpath from Birmingham to London, the M1 of the 1800's. I learnt lots about its history, so when I actually ran in the race I had highlights to look forward to and mentally cross off as I ran. I could think, 'Well, I know there's a unique tunnel at Shrewley, there's the flight of locks at Hatton called the 'Stairway to Heaven' and there's a massive tunnel at Blisworth to run over.'

All of that was interesting to me. It was like a framework that I could hang my race on. It's almost like I was buying into the experience of running the whole length of the canal.

Clocking up so many marathons does bring with it some bragging rights - I do love being able to impress folk with my running stats. I write a lot of emails to professionals, coaches, charities and so on and my credibility comes from my email signature which includes the number of marathons I have clocked to date - 1,000 is my target which I aim to achieve in 2017.

My running and coaching experience has also opened up a whole new world of opportunity for me… when I get people like Sir Ranulph Fiennes, 'The World's Greatest Living Explorer', contacting me for coaching it's immensely satisfying and a really surreal experience…

I was out running and my mobile rang - I always answer my 'phone because it's often a new client. Luckily I was at the top of a hill and the call provided a welcome rest. I answered and the voice at the other end said, 'Hello, Ranulph here. I've heard you're the go-to expert for the Marathon des Sables. Would you coach me for next year?'

Well, what do you say to that? It's the dream call isn't it? We arranged to meet at my home - this national treasure knocked on the front door… I let him in… he came into the kitchen and sort of said, 'Right, how do we go about this?' to which I replied, 'It's really easy, you just do as you're told.' 'Okay old chap, that's fine by me,' he said. And that's how we did it. That's the relationship we had. It was wonderful. When we went and ran 26.2 miles together, people were recognising him immediately and stopping him to take selfies. And while we were running along he told me in his own words some of his life stories. You can't get better than that.

At the time Sir Ranulph was 71 and the oldest British competitor ever to have run it. It was really important for him to finish because he was raising money for Marie Curie - a charity very close to his heart. He clocks up his fundraising like I am clocking up my marathon total - at the time of writing he has raised a staggering £16.3 million with a lifetime target of £20 million. But actually it was also really important for me that he finished the race and finished it in one piece - I didn't want him finished off on my watch. In one of her email messages out to him during the race, his wife wrote, 'Enough is enough - your daughter doesn't want you to return as a corpse.' Neither did I.

When celebrities walk through my front door it's like, 'Oh my God!' But you have to forget who they are and work out what help they need. Sir Ranulph was a 71-year-old guy that's had a double heart bypass, two heart attacks and survived cancer - he has to be careful, and I had to be careful with him. We've got the biggest single sand dune in the Northern Hemisphere down here in Merthyr Mawr near Bridgend in Wales - it's a 100-foot wall of sand. The command was simple - 'Up you go, Ranulph.' He was wearing a full oxygen face mask so I could measure his oxygen uptake on the wall of sand. Even the fittest guys blow out halfway up, but I stopped him near the top because I thought, 'My God - I'm going to kill him!' Most people don't have the same sort of drive as Sir Ranulph Fiennes - the man's got no 'off' button. His mind-set is fantastic - he's very, very strong and quite capable of banging his head against a brick wall for as long as is required - an essential quality for succeeding at ultra-running. With my help, he was prepared to put himself through pain until he got to the finish line.

The reason I'm so passionate about the time I spent coaching Sir Ranulph is that I could see we share this dogged determination to keep on going, to push through all those pain barriers to reach the ultimate ultra-racing finish line. And that's why I'm so drawn to the Marathon des Sables - it's the finish line to beat all finish lines. I love putting myself through it to reach that euphoric moment at the end when you finally achieve the goal you've been striving for - all those training runs, all that kit analysis, all that weight management - it's all worth it for that moment you run through the line and receive your medal from the Race Director - Patrick Bauer.

Waiting for the MdS in April every year is like it was for me as a child waiting for Christmas. The race fills up so quickly you have to enter at least a year in advance and the fees aren't cheap. The competitors have waited an eternity to get there - they've paid all the instalments, they've done all this training, they've bought the kit, they've been counting down the days and finally they arrive in the desert. Then, after a couple of days of packing and re-packing their kit, it's MdS Christmas Day!

At the Race Start you've got the buzz of the runners, you've got heavy rock music - Patrick Bauer always plays 'Highway to Hell' by AC/DC - and then the countdown. He shouts, 'Trois! Deux! Un!' The helicopter flies above us and all your hair stands on end. There's a huge cheer and everybody sets off at a crazy pace in over 50 degree heat, loaded down with giant rucksacks packed with their food and kit that has to last them the whole week of the race.

Then they find out what's really involved - it's harsh and it's brutal. It takes people up to and beyond their limits of endurance - some runners take all the skin off their feet whilst others collapse from hyperthermia. Blisters become a big problem for some people. In fact some of the blisters you see at the MdS are so deep that it takes months for the skin to grow back afterwards. This is generally caused by poor preparation, a lack of training, bad shoes and bad socks. Maybe back home that person is a high-flying executive - someone that can just afford to go and do this type of race… they sit at a desk all day and want to spice up their life a bit… they've seen it on the TV and they think it's the London Marathon in sand, but it's not. It's totally extreme and life threatening.

You must respect the distance you're covering - I have a

massive respect for the marathon distance. I can't afford to fail at the Marathon des Sables - it just isn't an option for me as it's my business, my livelihood: what would that do to my reputation?

No matter how many times you do the MdS, the thrill of taking part never diminishes. If you stand and put your hands up at the finish line you can actually feel the energy of the race. It's electric. You've got all these people crossing the finish line and Patrick Bauer is awarding them with their medals and kissing them on each cheek. He's a very spiritual guy who loves to race himself and he says congratulations to every single finisher.

Actually, even thinking about it makes me feel emotional. It makes me want to well up. It's just the best place on Earth; it's the spirit it creates, the memories; it's a culmination of a huge amount of effort. Just like when I finished my London to Lisbon Run at Euro 2004 and saw the corner of the National Stadium - my knees just buckled. Or when I ran the half-marathon at the end of my 28-in-28 in 2013 and hit the finish line after running 200 miles/week for four consecutive weeks. Or when I was greeted by Alan Shearer in the players' tunnel at St. James' Park at the end of my Premier League Run from Southampton to Newcastle visiting all the 20 Premier League grounds. Or when I got to the end of my first ultra in Grantham. I have relived that feeling over and over and over again. Maybe I'm just a running adrenaline junkie. I just love that feeling of crossing the finish line - that feeling of accomplishment.

And be it the Grantham Canal Run or the MdS, I'm always trying to recreate that feeling. So along with my marathon-a-week habit which started after that first Ultra in Grantham, I then signed on to do the Doncaster Doddle 42 mile Ultra in Yorkshire the following February. I planned to do this with my running mentor, John Martin, with whom I was still out running 20-milers every Saturday and Sunday. Training with John was like a musician doing the scales or the Karate Kid 'waxing on and waxing off' - running the 42 miles was going to be my 'live performance'. It was going to be like coming on stage at Wembley with 100,000 people in the audience, just like Freddie Mercury had done... That's still the thrill I get every time I run a marathon.

So John and I went through that autumn and winter season building up the mileage and I went and ran in the mud around Doncaster - 42 miles non-stop for 6 hours and 45 minutes - that was a really good time for the course and I finished quite high up in the field. I was in great shape and felt really confident. The next weekend, on 3rd March 1996, I went and ran my Marathon PB of 3:24:21 at the Borders Marathon in Suffolk. I was so well conditioned by this point that the race felt easy... and the conditions were far from ideal for running as the course was very rural and it was frosty. John had brought another friend from the running club with him but he was only doing the half. I thought, 'I reckon I can beat his mate in the half.' And I did! The course was two laps - I clocked 1:40 for the first and ran a slightly slower 1:44 on the second. But it didn't matter how cold it was or that I was wearing winter running gear as, with a mile to go, I was thinking, 'I really want to finish because I'm really starting to feel it now. I've given this everything I've got.' But I also thought, 'Keep the pace up Coleman as today is going to be a lifetime PB. This one's going on my headstone. And it doesn't matter if I can't walk or run ever again... Keep Going!' so I just carried on and ran myself into the deck.

And that race developed my theory on running PB's: it doesn't matter what the race is, how hot or cold it is, or whether it's hilly or flat - if you're going to run fast, you will. PB Days happen when all planets line up. Mine did for me that day.

It can happen when you least expect it. It did for me a couple of years ago when I ran the Mablethorpe Marathon. Mablethorpe is a seaside town near Skegness full of caravans and hordes of retired people. It's a place that time's forgotten. All the way there I was doubtful if it was going to be my day,

'I can't be bothered. I'll turn around and go home. Did I really need to do this today?'

When I got there it was absolutely thrashing it down with rain - I hate racing in the rain - so I got going and ran fast out of protest. But after 10 miles I was thinking, 'Good grief! I'm really going well here! It's still raining so the quicker I run, the sooner it'll be over.' And I just went and ran my quickest marathon for over 10 years. My planets lined up again and, like Bob Beamon's long jump record in 1968 or Paula Radcliffe's 2:15:25 at London 2003, I pushed myself to my limits.

Back in 1996 I wasn't just keen to improve my speed - I wanted to increase the distance too. Having completed the Doncaster Doddle 42-miler I set my sights on the annual 80 mile World Trail Championships on the South Downs. I'd spoken to a guy at my local running club who'd done it - he tried to put me off by telling me how hard it was. He'd told me how, at the halfway point, he had wanted to lie down and die. That got me thinking... 'I've done 42 miles and I didn't lie down and die then.' And then I thought some more... 'Actually, after I'd run 42 miles that day, could I have run another 42 miles?' And I decided, 'Well, yeah, I reckon I could have.' So I thought bugger him and went and did it anyway.

The race was incredibly hilly and the stretches on chalk were hideously hard. Being midsummers day it was also very hot and I tried not to let the sunburn cause too much of a distraction... then as day turned to night it became bitterly cold. Yet there I was, an ex-smoker-drinker fat guy, competing in the World Trail Running Championships. I bloody loved that race. I loved it even more when I finished in 16 hours and 43 minutes - 134th in the world! I thought, 'Hey that's pretty cool!'

I was now reaping the benefits of all the training I'd done throughout 1996. I went back and did races that I'd run before and bettered many of my times. My biggest achievement that year was completing the London to Brighton Road Race. It was inspiring to think I'd be running in the footsteps of many greats who'd gone before... Bruce Fordyce (one of the fantastic South African Comrades runners), Greg Dell, James Zarei and Mick McGeoch (one of my good friends with a 2:17 marathon PB) had all done it. And they'd clocked some amazing times.

So I lined up at the start thinking, 'Well, I'll just see if I can finish.'

Luckily there was an older runner there called Peter Sergeant. He was in his late sixties - he took one look at me and said, 'Are you alright son?'

And I replied, 'Yeah.'

He asked, 'First time?'

I said, 'Yeah, it is.'

To which he replied, 'Well, I've done the race lots of times before. The cut-off is 9 hours 30 minutes so if you finish in 9:30:01 there's no medal.'

That sounded a bit shit to me - to run all that way and not get a medal. I'd completed every race I had ever started, so I was thinking, 'God, that's a bit tight. And it's on the road.'

'Don't worry,' he said, 'Stick with me, and I'll get you there.'

So I thought, 'Sounds perfect.'

He was another John Martin. He had a million stories to tell about running and he'd run lots of other races in the Road Runners Book of Races. As we ran along together I just listened - he could talk as well as he could run. It was just like running with John at the weekends.

We started off right at the very back of the field and we just kept going. During those years of the race, if you stopped and walked, or if you were just going too slowly, there was a sweeper minibus. They'd stop and say, 'Right, in you get,' and pull you out of the race there and then. Walking just wasn't an option! As the day went on, true to Pete's word, we started overtaking lots of other runners, especially at some of the hills around the 30 and 42 mile marks where most people seemed to hit the wall.

People talk about 'hitting the wall' at London - at around 17 miles - but in ultra-running there are other walls further on. As you reach these distances you can actually watch runners start to wobble from side to side as their core muscles get tired. Nevertheless, we just started overtaking these people. The 'bus of doom' crept close at times and we could see the spent runners slumped inside the minibus.

At 48 miles, to add insult to injury, we had the Ditchling Beacon to contend with - it was a massive climb at this stage in the race. I just thought, 'Oh my God! We've just done 48 miles and now we're going up this massive mountain.' On the plus side, it was the one section of the race you were allowed to walk so it allowed a break from running - we speed-marched up to the top where it said, 'Welcome to Brighton.' Then it was time to start running again, and you're going, 'This is it! This is it! We're here! I know the race is supposed to be 55 miles but it says, 'Welcome to Brighton' on the sign - we've made it!'

Well, that sign is five miles from the bloody finish and you spend the next five miles running down into Brighton... looking at the time... looking at the time... thinking, 'How are we doing? How close to the cut off are we?' I'd been calculating our pace all the way and it was close.

We got there in a very relieved 9 hours and 26 minutes.

Of course that particular race time is etched in my memory forever, but I keep a record of every marathon/ultramarathon I've ever run in a giant excel spreadsheet. That spreadsheet is very important to me. From a performance perspective it's good to see my trends in race times but more importantly it's my history. It's a record of every achievement I've clocked on my way to reaching my ultimate lifetime goal of running 1,000 marathons... It's my chronology; it includes my world records and all of my running achievements; it's part of my private world which nobody else sees. It hides on my hard drive. And it's more than just a list of races to me… it's basically my equivalent of a diary… the number and genre of races I've done over the years paint my life story…

For example there are blips on my spreadsheet - times when I've been less active. If you check out 2005 and 2006 for instance… post-London to Lisbon in 2004… there aren't many marathons listed. At this stage in my running career I thought I'd climbed my Everest, performed my swansong. I thought that Lisbon was my epiphany, my crowning moment and my signing-off from running because I was getting older, I was re-married and I was having another child.

My thoughts at that point were, 'Well, I've done London to Lisbon. Maybe I should grow up a bit and not go running marathons all the time.' In actual fact 2005-2006 was a very weird period of time for me. I was a bit lost. I call it 'Neil Armstrong syndrome'. I had been given the moon… I'd been paid to run to Lisbon… I'd been on TV and I'd done all those incredible feats. But once you've done that, you go, 'Well, what's next?' It was like that for Neil Armstrong and proved to be a real living nightmare in his later life.

If you skip to 2008, however, you will find a lot more races listed - by then I knew that I needed to get back out there because it's my therapy and it's what I needed to do.

There are loads of races listed for 1998 too but for different reasons. There were still many exciting things to do on the horizon…

…Starting with my decision to run the Stratford Marathon and the London Marathon on the same day. It was a silly, fun thing I decided to do but I knew I'd have a blast doing it. The trouble was that in 1998, the Stratford and London Marathons were on the same day at the same time. I thought, 'If I do the Stratford Marathon early, I can run that, get in the car and drive to London, and then do the London.' So I contacted the organiser of the Stratford Marathon and said, 'I want to do it at midnight. I know the course, I know where it goes. Is that okay?' They said, 'Yeah, sure.'

So, at midnight, I went and jogged around Stratford, running a very comfortable race in 4:39 - nice and easy. Then I got into the car in my sweaty gear - there was no time for a shower - and drove flat out down the M40 in the middle of the night. I parked, hopped on a train and arrived at the start line in time for my second marathon of the day. To make matters even more enjoyable I actually did it with a friend of mine called Malcolm Bowyer. I'd met Malcy at the running club - he was the same age as me and great fun and I'd started running with him every morning. I used to knock on his door at 5:30am - very gently so I didn't wake up his family. We'd have a cup of tea afterwards and then I'd dart off to work. So we decided to do the double together and ITV came to film it for the news.

They made a huge feature of it on their programme as, at the time, not many people would have thought to have done this sort of thing. The two marathons were quite a contrast with just the two of us running in Stratford in the middle of the night, compared to London where there were 30,000 runners in the middle of the day amongst roaring crowds. We finished London a little quicker in 4:33.

I felt so fit. I'd run 3:36 the weekend before at the Taunton Marathon so this was dead easy. At this stage my running 'range' had gone into overdrive.

So what's 'range'? The best way to describe it is by using a driving analogy... I've been driving for over thirty years and I have built up enough experience to know that, if I'm going to drive to London, I'll look at the petrol gauge on my car. If it's full I know I can get there and back without having to stop to refuel. Running is the same... the more you run, the more you understand your body - you develop an intuition, a sixth sense - you reach a stage where you just know whether you can cover a said distance in a said time. I don't have to sit down and think for hours and hours wondering whether I can do something. I just know my range.

What does it feel like being this fit? I'd put it like this: if there's a brick wall, you can run straight through it. You feel invincible. For some people, though, they never feel that way. I'm coaching this lady at the moment - she's great, she's a really, really good runner, but she has zero confidence. It's a real shame and I'm working really hard to get her into my way of thinking...

And that's how I felt running Stratford and London back-to-back. It was great because we were running along with people that we'd not normally run with. I would normally have been running with the 3.5 hour runners - serious club runners. But for this London Marathon I was now running with the 4.5 hour runners - there were more fun runners around us. Running with Malcy was so much fun too as he's got such a good sense of humour. We loved saying, 'Well, you think you're struggling - we've already run the Stratford Marathon today!' And they'd go, 'You what?' So again it was, 'Ta da!' For me it was all about the 'Wow Factor'.

It was a great day out and at the end we got back in the car and drove home.

It wasn't until a few months later, whilst watching a TV item on a race in Morocco called the 'Marathon des Sables', that my world was truly turned upside down. I picked up the 'phone, called the organisers, paid my deposit and entered the race there and then.

And thus began my life-altering love affair with the heat, pain and wonderful hell of running in the Sahara Desert...

# CHAPTER FIVE

## THE MARATHON DES SABLES

### HIGHWAY TO HELL - AC/DC 1979

*If ever a race had a song that described it, the Aussie Rockers did just the job for the Marathon des Sables. I've lost count of the amount of times I've sung along to this classic in the start pen of the MdS while Race Director, Patrick Bauer, sang along in Franglais, 'Ighway to 'Ell.' I laugh every time it's played as it's so heartily sung along to before people are literally taken to hell and back. It was the last album featuring lead singer Bon Scott who died in 1980 from consuming too much alcohol. This seems quite poignant. It's possibly the best of all of the AC/DC anthems helped along by a huge dose of magic by Music Producer Robert 'Mutt' Lange.*

Back in 1999, the Marathon des Sables was still a well-kept secret in the running community. I'd read about Chris Moon MBE, a former soldier who very unfortunately became a lower-leg amputee in 1995 when he was blown up by a land mine in Mozambique. In 1997, just two years after this tragic incident, he ran the MdS with an artificial leg. He was, and still is, such an inspirational guy and in many ways is the original figurehead for Help for Heroes. He's certainly the guy that most land mine amputees looked up to for guidance.

In 1998, after reading about Chris' incredible efforts at

the MdS (and realising that we were actually the same age), one of my friends completed the race. I thought, 'That looks INCREDIBLE!' Not long afterwards, I was further bolstered by a sports programme I was watching on TV called Trans World Sport. It's shown on Channel 4 on Saturday mornings and always shows highlights from bizarre sporting events around the globe - the MdS just happened to be featured! I thought, 'I need to do that. I'M IN!'

By this stage I was a seasoned marathon runner having completed over 100 marathons in the previous year alone. Some of these had been very gruelling indeed, so I knew that I was suitably committed to the task ahead. I often returned from races completely wiped out - I raced hard seeking that euphoria of setting a new PB. Tough and mucky trail runs have always been my favourite - those two magic ingredients that both make you incredibly fit and also make you realise how fit you are. Experience is a major advantage in this sort of a race - even now I spend a lot of time overtaking people half my age, especially in the latter stages of races. There they are, all these running 'freshmen' wearing kit that's not appropriate for the job, and there's me, the old boy, blasting past. Don't get me wrong, we all have to start somewhere and that was me many years ago, but it's a bit of fun for the veteran in me!

So I immediately 'phoned Chris Lawrence, the UK co-ordinator of the MdS at that time: 'I've done 100 marathons this year,' I said. 'I really, really want to do this race.' The reception I received wasn't quite what I was expecting as Chris is a very honest and blunt kind of guy, 'I don't care how many marathons you've run in the UK,' came his reply, 'This is different. You're running in extreme heat, you're carrying a rucksack with all your provisions for the week and it is really going to take you to your limits!'

'It's going to test me?' I thought and smiled. Well, let me tell you, I loved the sound of that. So with my credit card in hand,

I hungrily read out the long number and signed up, there and then.

There was just one tiny problem - I knew nothing about what running this race entailed... absolutely nothing at all. I thought, 'Hey, it'll just be like running on the beach at Clacton-on-Sea, only a lot hotter.' I'd run marathons in the height of the UK summer which hadn't killed me yet, but not in the overwhelming heat of the Sahara.

Still, I was very much up for the challenge. So, in my innocence, I went and bought a giant rucksack from my local outdoor camping shop and filled it to the brim with all the different kinds of food I reckoned I'd need together with an assortment of pots and a huge cooking stove. Then I thought, 'I'll also go in fancy dress, why not?' After all, I'd run a few marathons in fancy dress up to this point with Big Dave - mainly the big city ones like London and New York. We'd had a complete ball - both of our outfits were made entirely from Union Jack material by my wife's sister who was a seamstress by trade - mine was a top hat and tails whereas Dave was a jester. So for the MdS, I thought I'd wear a lightweight desert version of that and jazz it up by carrying an eight foot pole with a massive Union Jack flag hoisted on the top. I felt sure it was in my range and was pretty gung-ho about doing it, because I was only 37 years old at the time, and super-fit. Armed with my costume and enough kit to break Buckaroo's back I headed to the airport.

I boarded the plane at Gatwick which was full to the brim with MdS participants. Our destination was Ouarzazate in Morocco, so for the next few hours there was a whole new crowd of people to talk to and find out what kind of running they'd done to prepare for the event. It meant I could ascertain whether they were more out of their comfort zone than I was and also gave me an opportunity to find seven other people to live with for the week. Eight people live together in a large open-sided Berber tent in a large circular chorale. It was like picking a football team back at primary school - joining up with people you liked the look of, assessing whether you could live with them.

The people I ended up sharing a tent with were amazing. I was with three Cambridge rowers who'd raced in the famous university boat race. There was a printer from Yorkshire who was of a very similar age to me and in a similar kind of lifeboat to me as he was divorced with three kids. Interestingly, there was also a lady married to a Greek businessman who said she was only doing the MdS to prove to him that she could do it. She was super-tough and carried on even though she'd broken a bone in her foot early in the race. The way people rebel against the negativity others bestow on them still fascinates me to this day. She smashed it and proved him wrong all the way to the finish!

So imagine the scene. It's the day before the race start and we're all sat in our tent chatting, wondering what to do with all this kit and food and all these energy powders we've brought with us... wondering what we should and shouldn't take. Then it dawned on me, 'Hold on, I'm carrying 13 kilos of equipment!' These days I take half that weight but it was my first MdS - I had no idea what to expect or what I'd need. This would be my baptism of fire.

And boy did I learn the hard way. Back then I didn't wear any sand gaiters - something everyone at the race now wears. This meant that every 400 yards in the dunes I'd have to take off my shoes to tip out the sand. I soon became desensitised to running with shoes full of sand and the distances between the tip outs got longer as the race went on. Nonetheless, I repeated this over and over again for 150 miles of the race which was totally tedious!

When I say I ran it, I really mean it: I ran that race! It was so liberating. As races go, it was a total revelation. My world at that moment changed from black and white to 4K colour vision. It was the same feeling I experienced when I saw a man land on the moon at the age of seven. The incredible desert landscape, the boiling temperatures, the way it stripped you down to your very core - it completely blew my mind. It didn't matter who you were, how much money you had or what you did for a living - you were completely stripped bare, turned inside out and turned back again. All you had to do was get from A to B... and survive! I'd found my place in the world.

After each day's running I'd head straight back to my tent - the people I was living with turned out to be even better than I'd first thought. They were lovely people who were just like me - they were positive, can-do people and they were there because they wanted to be there. We didn't get to know the other tents at all. It was just me and my tent buddies. These seven people became my support mechanism for the week - we shared a special 'Dunkirk Spirit'. There were foot problems in our tent too. One of the Cambridge rowers completely trashed his feet and they ballooned to the point where he couldn't even get them into his shoes on the last day. To add insult to injury, on the last morning one of the guys accidentally trod on his toes. The moment it happened his head practically went through the roof of the tent - he was in pure agony. That was just one of many typical moments that we experienced together in the tent and of course all but two of us split our sides laughing.

I also got to massage my ego a little bit while I was out there as ITV were making a documentary about the race. So as well as me having an amazing life experience, I even got to do my show pony bit in front of the cameras. They kept coming up to me and asking, 'So how's it going?' expecting to hear tales of woe and I'd just say, 'This is great, I'm loving it. It's fantastic!'

Remember this was my Christmas Day. I was living my very own heroic adventure out there. This was how the New Rory - the non-smoker, non-drinker - wanted to get his kicks. I was doing exactly what I wanted to do at that very moment in time. It was phenomenal. It made me reflect on how much I despised my old group of friends that enabled and encouraged me to go drinking with them. Out here I was free. I was also making it up as I went along which felt great as it was so spontaneous.

That's not to say there aren't a number of rules you must abide by whilst taking part in the race. For instance you have to carry 2,000 calories/day of food provisions - that's a whopping 14,000 calories of food you need to carry on Day One which means you have to be clever and carry very lightweight, energy-rich provisions. There's also a certain amount of compulsory kit you have to carry such as your sleeping bag (temperatures drop considerably during the night), a distress flare (in case you're just that - distressed) and, crucially, an anti-venom pump in case you're stung out there by a scorpion or spider so you can self-administer first aid until you get proper medical help.

In addition to the compulsory kit there are other things you might want to take such as a camera or a mobile. You have to weigh up all of these considerations very carefully during your race preparation. Over time I've managed to reduce my pack weight down to the minimum 6.5kg allowance but it takes experimentation and practice.

On top of that you've got to think about your running kit - what will you wear whilst crossing the desert? For me the decision was simple - everyone else seemed to compete in their regular running gear so I wanted to stand out from the crowd wearing my Union Jack outfit complete with flag. This added that extra stamp of toughness to my own personal race... gave it that extra oomph.

What I was thinking taking that massive cooking pot I'll never know. It was like something a character out of Blazing Saddles might use. Then of course there was the large cooker I took with huge blocks of hexamine - not only was it superfluous to requirements but, these days, it's considered so dangerous you're not even allowed to take something like that on the plane! Likewise, taking that eight foot pole with the Union Jack flag on top wasn't one of my better decisions, but it was one of my most fun - out of all of the 600 people competing at the MdS that year, I was the one that got noticed - and noticed to such an extent that to this day the organisers still refer to me as the nickname I was given that first year: 'The British Bulldog'. Even now the organisers say, 'Ah. Bonjour, Bulldog!'

Nothing can prepare you for the heat once you're out there running. The running distances at the MdS are generally broken down into four marathons over four days, with one 50-miler and then a shorter stage to finish. So for the day of the 50-miler, I ran half of it alongside a guy called Charlie who owned a milk farm in Sussex. He was running wearing a hat adorned with horns as a way of highlighting the Milk Marketing Board who'd sponsored him, and there was I in my Union Jack outfit. It was great just the two of us bounding along... until the sun set and we moved into the night section of the race. That was when it became a real physical and psychological test. In the dark you have no idea where you're going because all you can see is a disc of light on the floor from your head-torch. In reality you have no idea whatsoever where you are.

The experience of covering all this ground in the dark was bizarre. You relied on people manning the checkpoints to tell you how far you'd run, 'You're at 50 kilometres,' or even better, 'Welcome to 60 kilometres - keep going!' In the dark it feels endless - it's pitch black apart from other runners' torchlights and the lights you can see as you approach each checkpoint. The lights aren't always helpful - on the contrary they can be very misleading. You glimpse the lights and think, 'I'm nearly there!' An hour and a half later you're still going, 'I'm still nearly there, only it's not getting any fucking closer!'

The night section is part of the 'Black Magic' of the MdS though. Every 500 metres there's a glow stick attached to a post or a rock. The latter checkpoints actually shine a green laser along the route to the finish line which bends with the stratosphere. It's a real spectacle. One year, the moon was so bright that the whole deserted landscape in front of me was illuminated - there was a surreal bright lunar 'daylight'. I was running on my own so I turned off my head-torch and my only focus was the crunch-crunch-crunch of the gravelly sand beneath my feet. I was completely alone following the laser and felt totally at peace with the world. It was just me, running at ease, at ease with my life, at ease with the world, following the laser and following the markers. I had found my special place and moment in time. Ouarzazate, Merzouga, Tazzarine. These places in the Sahara Desert may mean nothing to most people - but to me they're the most special places on earth.

Meanwhile back in Charlie World, his sunburn was really beginning to get to him. He'd gotten severely sunburnt on the back of his legs during the day section so a medic had wrapped them up like a mummy, all the way from his ankles to his groin. Throw in the fact that he was also beginning to get very dehydrated and the stuff he started coming out with after about 26 miles was really very strange indeed. At one point he was talking about his death... I just thought, 'Well, we're going at about the same speed and he'll do as a companion to get through this section.' This might sound a bit callous, but back then we didn't have iPods to keep us going. In 1999 we still relied on CD Discmans and as they weren't an option, we all used each other to provide some form of entertainment.

My tent-mates, for example, all had a very diverse range of jobs which I learnt about. One guy was a computer expert; another was a lawyer whose main client was the British Government. I felt like I was a planet discovering all the other planets like me in our shared solar system. It was great to finally discover that there were other like-minded people, and here we all were together experiencing this adventure in the desert.

The MdS is always full of memorable characters. That year, there was a blind guy called Miles Hilton-Barber who spent the whole race climbing sand dunes and huge jebels with his guide, Steve Cook. It was amazing to witness. Steve would direct him over the sand and the mountains telling him exactly where he should tread and how fast he should run saying, 'Go up, go right, go left, go slow, mind that rock!' He had Miles on a leash like a dog for the entire race. Miles got the credit for completing the race, Steve got my credit for his selflessness as he had to manage everything for Miles 24/7 for the entire race.

Equally as extraordinary is Patrick Bauer, the Race Director. In the world of ultra-running he is simply God. He's a former French legionnaire who dreamt up the race and still directs it to this day. The MdS is his passion - even nowadays when there are 1,200 or more participants he always picks me out, says, 'Bonjour Rory!' and gives me a big bear hug and cheek-kisses like old friends do. Maybe part of my affection towards Patrick is based on gratitude. In my mind, it's like he created the race for me because it's given me the best personal and emotional moments of my life so far.

Maybe that's another aspect of the MdS which I treasure - the bond you develop with all the other characters out there who are experiencing the same things as you - the exhaustion, the feeling of accomplishment, the lows and the highs. Then there's the lack of facilities out there - you can't shower and you have a limited amount of water. The first time I completed the MdS, water was capped at 13.5 litres/day per runner. There were days when actually I didn't pee much at all because my body was trying to hold onto as much water as possible - I was totally dehydrated. The fact that I was also running in a cotton t-shirt didn't help and neither did the sub-par socks I was wearing. I had to customise my Union Jack Suit and Tails on the run too by taking off the buttons at the back with a penknife - they were beginning to rub my back under my heavy rucksack. That was what made the MdS special - making all these mistakes and then not even being able to brush your teeth, take a shower or have a shave in the desert. This was my apprenticeship. I loved learning on the hoof. I've never failed to get to the end of any race and that was my mentality back then. Throw me in at the deep end and I'll finish, I knew that.

Other runners out there that year weren't as open-minded as me - particularly when it came to one guy's snoring. His tent-mates said it was like sleeping next to a diesel generator and got so frustrated that they took all of his belongings and dumped them half a mile out in the desert. In fairness I had heard his snoring and it did sound like someone was doing some late night hoovering. It's a common problem out there - for some reason the snorers always seem to go to sleep first, so I'm told.

There's no question that spending all that time out in the desert has helped me to make my mind clearer. During those long, hot days of running I've realised that actually the things we cherish the most don't have a monetary value. I've learnt that money isn't important. I've learnt that my job isn't important, that possessions aren't important. You realise that people are important, as are relationships. It's thoughts like these that make the MdS my spiritual retreat.

Those 12 days at my first MdS gave me clarity. That's what makes me want to keep going back - to recapture that same feeling. I always say that people who do the race are either running towards something or they're running away from it. At my first MdS I was in the throes of going through a divorce from my first wife. It eventually led to me quitting my job which may have been highly paid but didn't give me satisfaction anymore. That's probably why I put so much into my first MdS. Other parts of my life were falling apart so I put more effort into the parts that weren't. The collapse of my marriage actually turned me into a better runner because when you're in a tough situation, going for a run makes you feel a whole lot better about yourself. By running across the desert and setting multiple running world records, as I did in that year before my first MdS, I was succeeding at something amidst some very dark times.

The MdS has had such a profound effect on me. It does every year yet when I'm back in the UK post event it feels like it was all a dream. I always get that strange feeling that the MdS is an imaginary world like the Enid Blyton story, The Faraway Tree. In this story lands revolve around a tree and the children go to different lands for different adventures. I'm here, right now, at my home in Cardiff, but how do I know Ouarzazate is still there? Is the desert still there when I'm here? Have I really done the MdS? It's like running but also it's like having been part of a fantasy too. Even now, when I watch videos of the race finish on YouTube for example, it strikes me profoundly, like, 'Gosh, there I am!' It's hard for me to explain that outer body worldliness that the MdS makes me feel, but it's also hard to grasp that it really exists. That's how surreal it is to run across sand dunes in brilliant moonlight with seemingly no-one else in the world.

Reaching the end of the race is also like an experience from another world. We ran into the town square of a place called Erfoud that year but no matter where the MdS finishes, the experience is always the same. You have your own euphoric moment as you cross the finish line and then you watch all the other competitors come in - it is unlike any other marathon finish imaginable. The finish at the London Marathon is great but the finish at the MdS is electric, literally. You can literally hold your hands up and feel the electricity; it makes my palms feel really hot. It is magical. Even describing it now makes me so emotional I feel like I'm going to well up at any moment. Every day of my working life clients say to me, 'Yes, but at the end, what's it like?' and I can try to describe it but it's like describing colour to a blind man. You have to see it for yourself. How hot is it? If you've got a fan oven, turn it up to 200° then open the door. It's unbelievably hot. How steep is it? Imagine climbing Mount Snowdon in Wales at over 1,000 metres, then imagine doing it three times whilst trying to cover 50 miles in one day carrying a 6kg rucksack. It's intense. And that's why I love it.

The first time I completed the MdS I found it very difficult to return home. I'd just been to the best party in the world and was coming home to... I don't know what. This is the state of mind I now refer to as 'Post-Traumatic Race Disorder'. Email was in its very early days back in 1999. It was a time when people used it more often than not just to send jokes. It was particularly thought-provoking, therefore, when one of the participants emailed all his fellow British competitors saying simply, 'Work is Shit.' Even more so when everyone replied in complete agreement. I felt the same.

I spent a month with my feet up on the desk. I didn't want to be back in the real world at all. I just wanted to be back in the desert. There was something deeper about being over there, something more real and far more spiritual. Back in the UK in my desk job world I had so many problems and concerns - my wife, the kids, money, everything it seemed. When I was in the desert it was all about running from A to B - all you needed was shelter at night plus enough water and food to keep you going. They were the only things you needed. Then you return home and... Whoomp! You collide with a massive wall of issues. I had to beaver away at things that no longer excited me and I had a real downer. I really missed the desert.

At work there were clients to deal with, at home there was maintenance to do as I'd been away. I remember I had to mow my garden lawn. Looking at it, I just stood there and thought, 'Why am I so keen to put stripes on it each time and make it look perfect?' That bemused me.

At lunchtime, I'd usually head across the busy High Street to Marks and Spencer but this time I thought, 'Why am I pressing this button to cross?' I stood and stared at it for ages then went back to work. That night I went shopping at the local supermarket, filled the trolley as usual but then froze in one of the aisles and just left it all there and went home. In Morocco, life was so much simpler. I had massive Post-Traumatic Race Disorder.

I'd returned from something totally unique and sublime and descended into a period of mourning. I needed a new challenge to give that same scintillating feeling of the MdS. I needed to run hard. I needed to push myself to the limit again. I needed an event that would test me... push me to the very upper echelons of my own limits. I needed to run on more sand.

# CHAPTER SIX

## BIGGER CHALLENGES

WELCOME TO THE MACHINE - PINK FLOYD 1975

*This is total 'Headphone Heaven' for me. The stereo effects are as alive today as they were some forty years ago. Hearing it now as it was recorded is simply amazing. The days of my Pioneer Cassette Deck, no matter how great I thought it was at the time, couldn't cope with the hiss even though it was Dolby C. I've always thought that life feels like being part of a machine and apart from being asked where you've been, you're asked what did you dream? That's a really important line for me as without a dream, well there's no vision and without a vision there's no direction, something that I can't live without.*

Anyone who trains for the Marathon des Sables ('MdS') is up for a challenge. It attracts all kinds of folk, although in my experience the majority of competitors are incredibly wealthy big fish in their respective ponds seeking a new way to test their inner self. It seems to be particularly appealing to those who are amidst a mid-life crisis, just like the one I had aged 31 back in 1994... most of my MdS clients are just turning 40.

A lot of people who come to see me for MdS coaching achieved a degree at University, got the Big Job, have their own PA and regularly jostle and fight their fellow executives for various perks and opportunities. They've reached a plateau where they earn a very comfortable amount of money but realise this isn't quite the epiphany they thought it would be and go, 'Oh, bugger this, I can't be bothered with this lark anymore.' Spiritually, that realisation leaves them feeling very frustrated. I have complete empathy for them as I've been there too, looking for a way out of my predicament. They've reached the point where they feel the need for a 'Life Laundry' in the sand.

The whole MdS process is a journey. You sign up, you train towards it, you get a new focus - it's not home, it's not the wife, it's not the family, it's not the business, it's not about money... it's not baggage. It is intensely personal. It is their time to live. It is their big 'Life Adventure'. And maybe it's the first time they've had the opportunity to be a bit selfish in ages and ages, maybe it's the first time they've had to fend for themselves.

Many of my clients are great runners. Many of them bust a gut to stay ahead of me, looking over their shoulder to see if they can beat me. That's just something you have to accept as a coach and of course realise that, if you have done your job properly, they should be beating you, sometimes by some margin. If you think about it, each year I've probably trained around 100 runners at the MdS, and I'm actually training them to beat me. That doesn't bother me though because for me, running is a big personal adventure - ultimately you're racing yourself. So when I run I always try to thrash myself out there, to put it all on the line. Otherwise, why am I going?

For other clients, however, taking on such a huge challenge with little or no extreme running experience proves to be most dangerous.

Only too often, my clients want me to transform them into experienced ultra-runners with the level of expertise required of them by the MdS in a very, very short space of time. Many give themselves just 12-24 weeks, but I've had people approach me as little as four weeks from race day. One of them was a lovely Welsh guy who 'phoned. He owned up straight away and said,

'I haven't done much. In fact, I'll be honest,' he said, 'I'm 40 and haven't done any exercise whatsoever in 20 years.' And he said, 'Just tell me what to do and tell me the right kit to take. I'll do whatever you say.'

And do you know what? In the race, he was absolutely brilliant because he just had this fantastic, sunny disposition. He knew he was going to get battered, stuck with it and got through. He was a lovely guy in fact and in a way, I really admired him. It's not a practise I'd recommend though so beware, as his feet hurt for weeks afterwards!

I'm honest with anyone that contacts me - I tell some people to defer their MdS entry for a year because they're nowhere near ready. I did it recently - I told my client, 'You're bonkers.' He said he wanted me to write him a training plan to include all his marathon races. I'd put all 14 of them into a 12-week plan, and simply said, 'I can't train you as there's no time for any training.' I can fast-track anyone, but there has to be some time for making improvements and for recovery. Running a marathon every week, weighing over 100kg, eating for Britain, he was all over the shop. But when I said to him, 'You're eating too much,' he was like, 'Really?' He was blissfully unaware that he wasn't helping himself. I told him to go away and have a re-think.

Another client this year, this time a lady, was too heavy when we first met. I had decided I would give her 12 weeks and then pass on the bad news as I was sure she didn't have what it takes. But, to my amazement, when we next met she'd stripped all the weight off. She'd really taken the training on board and could sense that she was going to be in trouble weighing that much, so she'd lost 14kg in 12 weeks - she'd dropped from 73kg down to 59kg! She totally transformed herself and looked amazing and years younger.

The heavier you are the slower the race is for you. That's why my first MdS was so enjoyable as I only weighed 77kg. My aim each year now is to be a similar weight, losing any excess gradually - it's just got to be that gentle downward trend towards race day, rather than stripping it off and then putting some of it back on again. It also helps to keep your focus during the whole of your training period, as that's the hard thing to maintain.

When I'm coaching I'm looking for trends. Life's about trends, isn't it? I'm looking for downward trends and upward trends, trying to find out what makes people tick and then getting them to stick to it. I like a few stats… not too many though just the basics - weight, pace, heartrate and 'miles covered' does the job. Any more than that and it's over-analysis time.

It works for my own training too as I like numbers. I'm good with them, remember them and juggle with them. They reinforce my beliefs and also provide me with a history I can look back on with great satisfaction and pride. The numbers jog the anecdotes, the memories, because life's a bit like riding a horse on a merry-go-round. You've got ups and downs and life is very rhythmical, isn't it? So, in more recent years, my own training has revolved around two goals - one in April for the MdS, and one in the autumn where I try to do a fast marathon. The rest of the time I spend recovering and then training for the next event.

The Druid Challenge has been a firm favourite in my running calendar for many years now - it's a great part of my business as well as being a hugely enjoyable event. I was the first over-50 there in 2013 which was really rewarding as I'd trained especially with that race in mind. In fact, since turning 50 my age has really worked in my favour as I'm now in the 50-59 racing category, separate to all the young bucks. I've achieved some pretty good results against people of a similar age to me. When I was 34, for example, my marathon PB was 3:24:21 so I'd come about top 2,000[th] out of 25,000 runners at the London Marathon. More recently I've done races where I've been in the Top 3 for my age category which is much more rewarding.

I digress! So my own first MdS experience dates back to 1999. Unlike many of my clients that I've coached for the race, I came back from Morocco feeling a little underwhelmed, like it wasn't the personal Mount Everest I thought it would be. It did have a huge impact on my outlook, but I don't think it was quite the physical summit I was hoping for. It certainly wasn't my swansong.

To make matters trickier, I had done the MdS whilst going through the process of a divorce. So when I returned home, I went to live with my parents for six weeks. At first, living with them again was fantastic but then they started killing me with kindness.

So there I am, a single man, living at the Hotel of Mum and Dad. It meant I could go and run anywhere, anywhere in the world, which is what I did. It was just like, 'Give me that road runners' book of porn - I'm going to do the lot!' My 'Life Laundry' at the MdS meant I had come back to a whole new home life... or rather lack of it.

I experienced 'Post-Traumatic Race Disorder'. I didn't have a home and I didn't have a wife. She actually remarried later that year and went to live in South Africa with her new husband, taking my three children with her. I had to sign a bit of paper permitting my children to go to South Africa - I knew that meant I wouldn't see them very often and that was extremely hard to come to terms with.

At my parents' home, meanwhile, it was just like being 16 again: cups of tea in bed in the morning, lots of home cooking and huge amounts of love and kindness. It was brilliant, but after a while you just go, 'Oh my God, all this kindness is going to kill me. I need to move out, for God's sake!' But my life was tinged by this sense of personal disaster - I'd failed at my marriage after 14 years, and when my children went my life had evaporated. I didn't live in the house that I'd been paying the mortgage on for years. I didn't have anything materialistic at all really except a sports bag with a few possessions and a small amount of money. That was it. I was stripped bare.

Nonetheless, what I did have was my fairly impressive career in marathon running. So what did I do? I said to myself, 'I'll go and run a load more! I'll go and acquire some more running world records, because when I did the last one I felt really good about myself.' So that's what I did. I came back from the MdS in 1999 and I actually signed up straight away for the MdS 2000 because I thought, 'I'll have another one of those, please.'

A month after I returned from the MdS, I did the Grand Union Canal Race for a second time. Then, even better than that, the organisers of the Marathon des Sables came up with a new race in Jordan called The Desert Cup. It started in Wadi Rum and crossed just over 100 miles of desert and mountains before finishing in Petra. They called it their 'Zero Edition' as it was a test run before they invited hundreds of runners to do it the following year for its proper First Edition.

Only 34 people ran it in total, with just two places for the English contingent. I was lucky enough to be given one of those places - maybe because I'd made an impression on them at the MdS and they knew I'd enjoy it. It was such an honour - I felt like I was representing Britain.

So there I am with Paul Shields, my MdS tent-mate, being greeted at Jordan's Amman Airport by a policeman holding a sign with 'Mr Colliman' in one hand and a machine gun in the other! Neither of us had the faintest idea what to expect so we just went with the flow into the Jordanian Desert for a week. Talk about extraordinary, fantastic and scary.

Before the start of the race we lived like an extended family in this giant tent in the middle of Wadi Rum where they filmed 'Lawrence of Arabia', with its spectacular pink sand.

It was truly beautiful in fact. The MdS is a huge rolling funfair of a camp - it's more like a village and is about the size of Wembley Stadium - it's huge. This, on the other hand, was really personal. It was just a giant tent and we all lived in it, race organisers included. It was really exciting, and because it was the 'Zero Edition' we were the pioneers of a whole new adventure. We were true explorers. Everything was unknown, the map and directions were a bit sketchy, and it was billed as being super-extreme. Game on…

I needed a totally different mentality for this race - I wanted to see how much distance I could handle in the extreme conditions - the heat of the desert combined with a –10° wind chill at night.

The first 60-odd miles were just sand. Endless fucking sand in fact and a complete ball-ache to get through. It just went on and on forever smashing your feet and destroying your spirit with every step. Then, with great relief, the sand finished but there was now a very steep 2,500ft climb up into the mountains. It finished with a painful descent down 540 steps into Petra - the ancient lost city where one of the Indiana Jones movies was filmed. In total, the race took me a colossal 43 hours and 23 minutes. It just took ages! And I hadn't really had a break from running leading up to the event - I'd recently run both the Chicago and New York City Marathons, yo-yoing across the Atlantic to run marathons in the UK in-between, all in the four weeks leading up to the race. I was hooked on that feeling of accomplishment.

Would I taper now? Yes, for big races. Did I do it then? No. I just went and ran. Your perspective changes as you get older - you focus more on your longevity in the sport. Back then I was purely into quantity, and spending as much time as I possibly could in my therapeutic running bubble.

That said, all those marathons in the lead up to The Desert Cup had made me faster and fitter. I'd done the Robin Hood Marathon in 3:32 and the 55 mile London to Brighton on the road in 8:55. In fact I'd run 86 marathons that year so I was super, super-fit and headed off to Jordan feeling bullet proof.

Luckily, one of the runners was a lady called Anke Molkenthin from Germany (she's actually won the MdS) who somehow seemed to know the way. I, on the other hand, didn't have a bloody clue where we were going! We passed through Jordanian towns and villages, following little red arrows on the ground, but she seemed to be really good at knowing where we were headed. So I thought, 'Right - that's it. I'll just keep up with her.'

Better still, she'd also done a lot of desert races so she was far more experienced than me, but thankfully she wasn't quicker. It was great... over that distance, I was about the same speed as her and we just trotted along nicely together.

It was a bizarre race. In the middle of this vast expanse of desert, there was a railway line. A single-track railway. We knew it was coming up and knew it was ahead of us for a long time. Nothing travelled along it for hours yet just as we went to cross it a train came along. It was like - what are the chances of meeting a train in the middle of the desert on this isolated track in the middle of nowhere? So we actually had to stop and wait for it to go by - and it was one of these mile-long beasts with lots of industrial carriages on it. I did the race the following year and exactly the same thing happened - such a ridiculous coincidence!

We continued on, in the middle of the night, passing through towns, dry river beds and natural arches of rock - you've got these big buttresses that stick out from the end of spurs of rock which are natural phenomena, but they look like they've been melted with a blowtorch. It was magical.

At 4:00am it's not as romantic as it sounds and I ran on ahead of Anke. As I entered Petra I ran with all my valuables in my hands - I had my money, passport, camera, everything as I thought I was bound to get robbed, especially given that the paranoia had really set in by this point as I'd been awake for so long. Can you imagine running through the Indiana Jones set at 4:00am? There was no-one there, although being so tired

I was absolutely convinced that I could see eyes looking at me from the shadows! Was I scared? I was petrified! However I was over the moon and felt triumphant at the finish.

I went back the next year for the First Edition of the race. I ran a lot of it with a guy called Andy Blackford. He's the guy that used to write the funny last page in 'Runner's World' magazine each month and he had an endless supply of life stories to fill the hours and hours of running. His, 'I played lead guitar with Thin Lizzy,' stopped me in my tracks. 'Sorry, you what Andy?' I said, 'Yeah, I actually played lead guitar with Thin Lizzy for a week when they were choosing a new guitar line-up and it came down to either Scott Gorham and Gary Moore or Me,' he qualified. He continued that his band had supported Genesis in the mid-seventies, and they'd been out to where Genesis had recorded the 'The Lamb Lies Down on Broadway' - one of my all-time favourite albums. My running had taken me back full circle to 1974.

But, magical moments aside, this race took me right out of my comfort zone. I'm not kidding, it was scary. Between the checkpoints, technically, we were lost. If I went back and did the race now, I wouldn't be so scared because I've done lots of other audacious races since then. But at the time, here I am, just a little lad from Stratford-upon-Avon that used to drink and smoke, and I'm now running across the Jordanian desert in the middle of the night. It's like, 'Shit!'

And that's before you factor in the dogs. There were loads of the buggers! Horrible, vicious dogs running wild in the little towns which we passed through. So I wasn't very happy about that as these dogs were growling with their hackles up. I was thinking, 'I've got to brave it out. I want to get to the finish line... I want to get the medal...' I felt like I was representing my country, I'd never failed at any running challenge and I was out doing what I wanted to do. So it was a case of telling myself, 'Toughen up buttercup, forget the dogs and get on with it.'

And not only was I desperate to finish, I was also there trying to build a new future for myself. I thought, 'Okay, what am I going to do with my life? Is my new mission in life going to be running super-length marathons? I'm now like this desert warrior... I've run across the Sahara Desert... and I'm doing lots of new things that other people haven't done before. I was one of only two people in the UK that had ever run this race in Jordan. That made me super-elite again. I liked that as I like being at the top of the pyramid.

The Desert Cup enabled me to put into practice and build upon everything I'd learnt at the MdS - looking after your feet, making sure you've got the right shoes, wearing gaiters to avoid sand getting into your trainers, minimising the equipment you carry, and so on.

The whole event, if you can call it that, was so stripped back, so unchartered, so raw. It was like, 'Wow - this is MdS to the power of 10.' The MdS was my launch; the Desert Cup was my successful sequel... my great follow-up single... my French Connection II. But where do you go after that?

Following The Desert Cup I went back to run the MdS in 2000 because I wanted to drink from the MdS cup of desert fantasy once more. Much like the first time, it didn't tick all the boxes - that realisation was soul-shattering. It was incredibly hot that year - around 60° in the dunes. But it just wasn't the ultimate challenge I was seeking.

After that I didn't go back to the MdS again for a long, long time. I did other stuff because I found out that, okay, it's billed as being the world's toughest footrace - maybe it is, maybe it isn't - but it wasn't my toughest footrace. I had to go and find a bigger challenge.

That was when I realised that I had to actually go and find and set my own goals because I couldn't find a race that fit the bill. It made me realise that I needed to go back to the basics of running, to work out why I enjoyed this sport in the first place.

And so for the next two to three years I searched for the answer. I couldn't find what I was looking for. I was still pushing myself athletically but I felt stagnant.

It was against this backdrop that I met and married my second wife. We'd met in a professional capacity because I'd been running marathons to raise money for Help the Aged and she worked for the charity's Press and Media. Unfortunately, I found that the new relationship had a detrimental effect on my running. I certainly wasn't going out and doing the 86 marathons I did the year before. So maybe it deflected my running. It certainly curtailed it because I wanted to put a lot of effort into my new relationship and because maybe I hadn't put the same amount of effort into my previous relationship, especially towards the end of it.

Spiritually it left me feeling spread far too thinly. To make up for it I began cherry-picking races - I did The Desert Cup again. In between those races, however, I didn't run as many marathons as I wanted to in order to spend more time with my new wife.

I wanted to be successful in a marriage. I'd been very unsuccessful towards the end of my first one and I wanted to see if I could actually make a good go of it. I soon realised, however, that it would be impossible to become a master of both worlds. You can either do one or the other. Or at least that's what I thought until I met my current (third) wife. She's a runner - we actually met at the MdS a few years ago and it's a totally different dynamic because as runners we understand what makes each other tick.

Between 2000 and 2002 I was in a running rut - I was in the wilderness. I felt more and more frustrated. But I think that's natural in life. You start a new relationship, you get married, you buy a new home - and it's not an unpleasant experience, it's just different to what you've been used to.

Somehow I was now back in that same position I found

myself in after my first MdS, wondering why on earth I was stood in my garden putting stripes on my lawn. What was the point of it all? What was everything in aid of? Then suddenly I did a, '1-2-3, wake up, Rory, you're back in the room,' and decided I needed to go and do some more running.

Part of the problem was that I had moved from Stratford-upon-Avon to Nottingham where my new wife lived. That meant getting a new job, any job, to keep some money coming in. So I ended up going back into the print industry but into a role way inferior to where I had been before. I got a job as an estimator at a printing company and it was the worst job in the world. So mind-numbingly boring. I started off running 6.5 miles into work in the mornings and running 6.5 miles home in the evenings to give me that running buzz. After a couple of months, however, the job became so soul-destroying that I couldn't muster the enthusiasm to run there anymore. So I bought a car. I thought, 'I just can't run there ever again as it just doesn't fire my imagination'.

So my life was spinning out of control again - I was stuck in a job I hated and was not able to do the one thing I was truly passionate about, running.

In 2002 I staged a mini fight-back. I tried to rekindle the Running Rory of old with a running pilgrimage. This meant running to every Premier League Football Ground in England.

It was time to raise the bar - in spectacular style...

# CHAPTER SEVEN

## MEGA-DAY RUNNING

### INSIDE OUT (LIVE) - PHIL COLLINS 1985

*Phil Collins is at his best with this mid-eighties classic. Only ten years prior to this he was drumming on the classic 'The Lamb Lies Down on Broadway' double Genesis Album. Here he's Producer, Song-writer, Pianist and Drummer surrounded by a great live act including Chester Thompson on Drums and Daryl Stuermer on lead guitar. The lead solo is one of my favourites of all time because it's so well-crafted. Funnily enough, Peter Gabriel is on backing vocals. Talk about full circle!*

Whenever people question whether they're too old to take up running, I always think of Sir Ranulph Fiennes. As his running coach for the MdS in 2015 he just blew my mind: how many 70-year-olds do you know who can go jogging for a marathon distance in the middle of the countryside in training?

And yet he's a shining example to all of us that anyone can do it. You just have to put your running shoes on and get out there and do it. Sir Ranulph is someone who relishes a big challenge - he's 100% committed and can spend all day at the coalface as long as he's climbing Everest or walking to the South Pole. Give him a bitesize task and he's not interested. This meant he had the perfect mind-set for tackling the ultimate ultra-running challenge that is the Marathon des Sables.

*Christmas 1993*

*Middlekerke Marathon -1997*

*Desert Cup - 1999*

*Flora London Marathon - 1997*

*London 2 Lisbon, Heaven - 2004*

*London 2 Lisbon, Motorhome - 2004*

*London 2 Lisbon, Finish - 2004*

*Marathon des Sables - 2011*

*Avebury - 2014*

Stoptober, Trafalgar Square - 2013

Marathon des Sables with
Ranulph Fiennes - 2015

*Coach Coleman*

During the time I spent coaching Sir Ranulph I learned the importance of longevity - like him, I also want to be doing this when I'm 70 which at the time of writing is only 16 years away. I've already been running ultras for 22 years, so if I can keep going for another 20 at least and continue to experience as much enjoyment from them, I'll be a very happy man. Maybe I'll just get to a point where I go, 'Do I need to do this anymore?' Sir Ranulph obviously hasn't reached that stage yet - he still hasn't written the last chapter of his book.

My parents got married very young. They are both now in their 80's and recently celebrated their 60th wedding anniversary. It was amazing to hear them share their thoughts and experiences from the 60 years they have spent together... about the love they've had, the times they've shared, the children they've brought into the world. It's an amazing partnership and they still walk around the supermarket together holding hands - it's dead cute. But they're ten years older than Sir Ranulph and they certainly couldn't run 26.2 miles...

At some point in my life I'm going to have to accept that I'm going to reach my ultimate brick wall where I won't be able to run marathons any longer. Hopefully I have plenty more to come yet though and Sir Ranulph certainly influenced me in terms of being more astute about the challenges I take on. So if there's a challenge, make sure it's a good one - that's what he does. He only does BIG stuff. A great philosophy of his is that, 'No-one is interested in who came second.'

Maybe as you get older it's a bit like a Led Zeppelin comeback. They didn't start with a few small gigs - they went straight back in at the big time playing at the O2. So for me, if I'm going to take on a challenge - Bang! I do it big. And I don't spread myself too thinly so that I can remain focused on the task in hand. I think about my running style - I run with a lot of energy economy... that's what I've instilled in Sir Ranulph. He refers to his running style as a 'shuffle' - it's not a shuffle, actually. In fact I think he has a certain amount of modesty about what he does - he can trundle along quite nicely and very economically when he wants to.

So, for me, once or twice a year I'll pick a big race and really put a lot into it. I'll think about it for weeks, I'll carbo-load and, when I get there, I'll run it very hard - as hard as I can. It's about me focusing on me. A few years ago I was challenged by my good friend Mick McGeoch to run his legendary Barry 40 race. It's 161 laps of a 400 metre track and a mind boggling prospect but I was totally inward focused and ran it hard all the way leaving the outside world as a blur for all 6 hours and 19 minutes.

It's the focus that drives my running, and as previously mentioned it's what I lost around the millennium when I got caught up making a home and a new life with a new wife and children. I was constantly renovating the house and redoing the garden and got side-tracked into living an average sort of life. I broke free in 2002 when I ran to all the Premier League grounds in Britain - the 660 miles from Southampton FC to Newcastle United FC worked quite nicely. I wasn't focusing on setting big records - I'd done nine treadmill world records so I'd made my mark on the running world. As soon as they became public knowledge every man and his dog took it upon themselves to go one better and beat them. I could have gone back and beaten them again but then you're in danger of getting caught in a never-ending cycle of retaining your records.

I've done that chapter in my life. The world records fulfilled my need at the time for another 'Everest' but I wanted to move on from that.

Instead, I started looking at the idea of 'a running pilgrimage', a concept that gradually became more and more compelling. So if you go and do, say, the London Marathon - the race goes from A to B. It starts at Greenwich Park and finishes at the Mall. So you've got this fantastic journey going from place to place. If you run a marathon that starts and finishes in the same place, you expend a huge amount of energy only to end up back where you started hours earlier. I was getting the feeling of, 'Well, why have I done that?' I'd been to places but I hadn't travelled anywhere.

So the idea of a journey from Southampton to Newcastle really excited me. It worked really well, actually, because I did it with a charity called Quit, whose message is to support people who want to stop smoking. The run was a perfect outreach to footie fans who wanted to 'Quit' their nicotine habit and I was the perfect example of being a super-fit ex-smoker.

I was started off at Southampton FC by their manager at the time - Gordon Strachan. When I explained what I was doing, he just said, 'You're fucking mad, off you go.' Sir Bobby Charlton was far more encouraging when I met him later on in the challenge and I was very lucky to run out onto the pitch at Old Trafford, which was just an amazing experience. I finished the run at Newcastle FC, running onto the pitch with Alan Shearer on match day to celebrate the 660 miles I had covered running a marathon a day. It really was a premier run for me. A complete eye-opener of what I was capable of.

The run was meticulously organised. We stayed in hotels each night so I'd get dropped off each morning, run 26.2 miles, mark where I'd finished, and then start again the next day.

Luckily we had a food sponsor deal with Pizza Hut for the run, so at the time we could eat whatever we wanted but it had to be Pizza Hut food. Consequently, I could actually list the Pizza Hut menu off by heart and haven't been back since! Nonetheless, during the run it was great because you could go in and stock up on pasta and pizza on their 'all you can eat' deal.

I knew with my baseline fitness that 660 miles was more than doable - all I had to do was jog marathons out, one after another after another, day after day - not fast, just steady. I had absolute belief in my ability to complete the task.

I never questioned that belief. That's the thing about having this range of fitness from going to all these various places and doing 'big stuff'. When I'm at peak fitness I know that if I had to, I could trot out 26.2 miles a day indefinitely.

In fact, there's a coast to coast race across the States that's 140 back-to-back marathons. The likelihood of there ever being an opportunity to take this much time out is pretty remote, but never say never as I know I would really enjoy the journey. It would be a great way to see the USA and one hell of a journey. I did email the organisers, told them my story and said, 'Can you give me some more details?' And they just said, 'Yeah, you'll be all right.'

When I did the Premier League grounds, it was the landmarks and the stats that I focused on. I visited all the London stadia in one day - they were like checkpoints in a race. Everton and Liverpool were the closest to each other being less than a mile apart. From Liverpool, however, it was up to Manchester United and then on to Blackburn via the Langworthy Road out of Manchester - now that's a really tough neighbourhood.

Many of the runs on this journey coincided with match days and culminated with a run onto the pitch before kick-off. On these days, to highlight Quit and my principle sponsor Nicorette, there was a man with his face painted white dressed in a giant cigarette costume. The cigarette was about three metres tall and looked like a giant B&H, and it ran out onto the middle of the pitch at half-time. The ball boys or the apprentice footballers would then follow armed with these big 'Nicorette' branded white cushions that represented giant Nicorette chewing gums. They would chase the cigarette around the pitch and then stub it out with the cushions. It amused the crowd anyway and as I ran around the pitch I was showered with cigarettes!

I met Sir Bobby Charlton on match day at Leicester City's Filbert Street Ground. It was one of the last games ever to be played there before moving to their new King Power Stadium.

He's got quite a nice Geordie accent. He asked, 'What are you doing, lad?' So I proudly replied, 'Well, I'm running to all the Premier League grounds. I'll see you at Old Trafford in a few days.' With eyebrows raised, he wished me good luck. Sir Bobby Charlton was a childhood hero. He was a sticker in my 'Soccer Stars in Action - 1970' album, and here I was talking to the real life version. Some of his goals are etched in my mind as he scored some real thunderbolts, and here he was in front of me. It was like meeting footballing royalty.

On my journey I also met Pat Jennings, Martin Chivers and Martin Peters - players I'd watched as a child - football was a popular sport in my family and Saturday night was 'Match of the Day' night.

My Premier League run was a mixture of 28 marathons and ultra-marathons. As for some of the roads I ran up...! Running on the hard shoulder of the A38 dual-carriageway from Aston Villa to Derby without a pavement was particularly dangerous. But the interesting thing was that I was fear free because it was an adventure, and if you've got an adventure and if you've got this target that you're going to achieve, you don't think about fear as your ambition drives you on. My only thought was to get to Newcastle because the BBC were there waiting to hear my story.

I do love involving the press when I'm taking on a new challenge. There are usually two focal points to any big run - the first being, 'I'm going to go and do this run.' People are generally pretty dumbfounded... 'Wow! That's amazing! Really? Where are you going to go? What are you going to do? Are you going to make it?' Then there's usually a bit of a lull whilst you're on the run - it's actually a bit of a non-story. Once you've finished, however, that's when you get the adulation. That's when people say, 'Oh my God! What an amazing feat!' I was super-proud to finish this run standing with Alan Shearer in the players' tunnel. It was the last Newcastle home game of the season and I ran out onto the pitch with the players.

Looking back, when it came to my preparation there was a beautiful simplicity to it. Forget carbo-loading. I didn't really have to pluck up courage to do it - I just got up and got on with it. I knew I had that baseline of fitness so I tapered down with a couple of marathons and before I knew it, it was March and I was bang on schedule reaching all of the Premier League grounds before the end of the season.

For me, at that particular moment in time, this was the most important thing in my life. I didn't think to myself, 'I can't do this,' or, 'I've set myself an impossible challenge,' because failure was not an option.

In fact I was actually planning to do it again in 2013. Teams had been promoted and relegated so it would have been a different route - I was going to start at Newcastle and run south this time, finishing one mile from home at Cardiff City's Stadium. Somehow though I just couldn't get the logistics sorted out in time and shelved the idea. Sometimes you plan things and then they don't come off. But that's okay - you can't win all the time, can you? Cardiff City were relegated at the end of that season so it's on hold until they are back in the Premiership. Hopefully it won't be too long a wait!

Once my Premier League run was in the bag I was keen to start planning my next challenge. It was then that I spotted an article in The Daily Mail which really floated my boat! David Bedford (former race director of the London Marathon) and a colleague of his, Peter Radford, were organising a super-tough challenge which I wanted to be a part of...

I had met David Bedford a while back when I was clocking up my treadmill world records. It turns out that he had been out for a boozy lunch with Peter who had written a book about Captain Robert Allardice Barclay, famed for covering one mile every hour for 1,000 hours back in 1803. Back in Barclay's time, there was a gambling pursuit called pedestrianism which attracted huge amounts of money. Barclay reputedly made £320 million (in 2003 equivalent terms) from the Prince Regent for completing this challenge.

So, over lunch, Bedford and Radford came up with the idea of reliving the 'Captain Barclay Challenge' as a pre-London Marathon media campaign… for every hour of the day, 24 hours a day, competitors would have to get up, run, walk or crawl one mile, and then wait until the next hour and do it again. And so was born the 'Flora 1,000 Mile Challenge'. They were seeking six people to take it on and as soon as that advertisement appeared in the Daily Mail I was inundated with telephone calls… 'Have you seen this? I think you ought to do it.'

I contacted the London Marathon Office and 170 people were shortlisted. It was a bit like 'The X Factor'. The numbers were slowly whittled down and we all met at a gym where we went through a series of fitness and psychometric tests to assess our interpersonal skills and ascertain whether we could cope with living in a confined space. Next we were assessed for our current media exposure and our ability to come across well on camera in press and media interviews. The finale was at the Tower Thistle Hotel near the Tower Bridge. David Bedford 'phoned me in my room and said, 'Final question, why should I pick you?' And I said calmly, 'Dave, you've got six people doing this. Obviously it's cost a lot of money to put on this challenge and you need somebody to finish.' I said, 'I know that at the end of it, I'll still be going.' And he said, 'Right, you're in. And you'd bloody well better be.'

The event was organised such that the 1,000 miles would finish in the hour preceding the London Marathon, following which we would run the London Marathon. So the goal was actually to run 1,026.2 miles in six weeks.

We lived on one of those rock 'n' roll sleeper tour buses complete with lounge, kitchen and bunks of course. The final six comprised two girls and four guys and we were even paid - £7,000 for the 1,000 mile feat and a further £1,000 bonus if you then successfully completed the London Marathon. Best of all it was tax-free as it was considered race winnings. I felt like a pro-athlete getting paid to run the London Marathon!

The tour bus we lived on moved up and down the London Marathon course whilst we were out running. This would typically be from just before until just after the hour was up, allowing for a 70 minute sleep in the middle. Originally, when Captain Barclay had done the challenge on Newmarket Heath, he'd walked out to a post and then back. For us, however, the idea was that this was a round-the-clock moving media campaign using the whole London Marathon course from start to finish to start to finish and so on.

Prince Andrew started us off at four o'clock on a Sunday afternoon from Buckingham Palace. Hazel Irvine, the BBC commentator from 'Grandstand', was there. We were live on TV, and every week she'd come out to see how we were getting on - we were marathon running heroes in the press.

Our experience was a far cry from that of Captain Barclay! According to his original notes he'd had a pretty tough time - he got drenched in the rain which meant he became very cold and contracted rheumatic fever just eight days in. He also lost an enormous amount of weight. Back in 1803 there wasn't free access to clean drinking water so they used to drink beer - it was very weak but nonetheless, he was drinking quarts of the stuff every day! And towards the end of his challenge, because so much money was at stake, he was actually accompanied by an armed guard to protect him and his winnings.

My challenge wasn't risky in terms of money but given the unknown nature of the challenge we all had concerns... How would our bodies react? Would pain set in? Would we lose an enormous amount of weight? In response to this last question I started eating two curries a day! There was also a pie and mash shop in Greenwich near the 'Cutty Sark' which I passed at least once a day and stocked up on a couple of pies and extra mash if

I still felt peckish. After a week I was about a stone heavier, so I thought, 'Maybe I need to be a bit more scientific with my diet,' and cut the calories from then on to match my output.

The other big unknown was sleep disruption - we only got about 70 minutes of sleep at a time so it was a bit like having a new-born baby - we didn't get any deep REM sleep just lots of light dozing. So although we thought we were acting perfectly normally, actually we weren't.

Towards the end of the six weeks I was actually starting to go slightly bonkers - I started to have some very strange thought patterns. It was definitely more of a mental challenge than a physical one for me. So for the last week or so I decided to sleep as much as I could to fritter away the time. It turned out that I went to sleep over 300 times in the 42 days and I could literally count back 3-2-1 and drop off immediately.

Press and the media were fairly integral to the whole event - all six of us attended media training courses to ensure that we could speak live on TV and Radio without making an embarrassment of ourselves or the London Marathon organisers. During the final week, the challenge moved indoors to the London Arena where race registration was held for the London Marathon. That meant everyone who ran the race that year looked on whilst they collected their race numbers. It felt very special indeed. It also coincided with the explosion of the Internet so people could follow us online and ask us questions. It really was ground breaking.

The icing on the cake was that this was the year when Paula Radcliffe set her amazing world record of 2:15:25. So the next morning I was lucky enough to attend the same press conference as her and felt incredibly privileged to be stood next to her during the photoshoot as, in my opinion, she's the greatest distance runner of all time. Why? Well, set your treadmill to 18.6kph and run on it for 2 hours and 15 minutes. It's an extraordinary achievement.

How did it compare to the year before when I'd done the Premiership grounds? Well this was in a league of its own as we had massive media coverage backed by the London Marathon and the BBC - in the days and weeks that followed the Flora 1,000 Mile Challenge, The Daily Mail ran individual features, 'Runner's World' went into overdrive and the BBC ran news updates. New stories also appeared on 'Grandstand'. The whole experience just totally pumped me up.

That said I did take a lot of time off after the event. The thing was, at the time I didn't realise just how much it was destroying my body. Mega-day challenges do destroy your body, and to a certain extent they destroy your mind as well. You need to take some time out - to have some space. It's a bit like childbirth - you have a child and for the first six months you don't know what day it is! It did feel a bit like that in April 2003. I went and did some regular marathons and they were taking me well over four hours to complete. The Robin Hood Marathon had previously taken me 3.5 hours and it was now taking me five!

I found it really hard to summon up the energy and the effort to run fast around Nottingham in a big loop only to finish where you had started. It was hard to adjust from being a superstar in the Flora 1,000 Mile Challenge. I imagine it's a bit like being a recording artist that's lost his label - you just become a washed-up has-been, perhaps. I'd once said that if I ever ran over four hours for a marathon I'd pack up, so I was really letting myself down. Maybe I was just running these marathons in the hope that they would rekindle my passion for running and let me relive how I felt doing the Flora 1,000 Mile Challenge.

At the time I didn't have a clue why I felt like this - I was just floating in space in some kind of lost time. The thing that kept me afloat psychologically was that I was continuing to rack up my marathons - I was nearing the 500 mark. Marathon 500 was something to look forward to. There were very, very few people worldwide at that time who'd clocked that many so maybe it was a question of, 'Well, I'm just going to clock the numbers, and maybe that's going to tick all my boxes.'

Then Lady Luck shone down on me again - Gillette were looking for somebody to run to Lisbon in 2004 to promote their Rightguard Extreme advertising concept by tying it into the Euro 2004 Football Championships. They had been looking fruitlessly for someone suitable for about 18 months and in desperation they telephoned the London Marathon press office and got the answer, 'Call Rory Coleman - he'll do it.'

'We need someone to run to Lisbon. Can you do it?' was all that they asked. I simply replied, 'Yeah!' I wasn't interested in the logistics, how far it was, or anything else for that matter! It was a good job really as they didn't have a clue themselves - they were under the impression it would be around 10 miles a day which they viewed as pretty extreme to do day after day. But I knew it was more than that, so I consulted my AA Europe Route-Finder map - in those days you couldn't just Google it online. Then I loaded it onto my computer and did the calculations: it was 1,275 miles which is exactly 2,004km - pretty ironic given the year of the run.

The call from nowhere had ripped me out of my rut, out of the tailspin - it was a life-saver! 'Would you like to run to Lisbon?'

And I'm like, 'Yes please!'

Then came the Brucie Bonus, 'And we're going to pay you to do it.'

'Even better!'

And that was the start of my next adventure... it's funny - I've got really rose-tinted glasses when I reflect on my running career. I only ever see the highs. When you think about it in more depth, however, you realise that there were also a number of lows there too. I've found out that it's not just about the successes but how you conquer adversity - remaining positive and focused both in life and in running has given me a real edge. It's a personality trait of mine that I'm proud of and is something I also saw in Sir Ranulph Fiennes. It took him three attempts to conquer Everest - he remembers the one he made the summit, the others are forgotten.

I had a lot of successes in the nineties and I really enjoyed those first few years of training for fitness and challenging myself. But really, when I reflect on my journey, those running successes took place against a backdrop of some serious life issues. Maybe my highs and lows in running inversely mirror those that take place in my personal life. When I seem to be at my most miserable in my personal life, I seem to be doing my best with my running. So maybe the low points trigger my running power.

In my experience, when life starts to run away with you and you begin to feel a bit out of control, you channel your energy into something you can control and be proud of. So when my world has been turned upside down, I've decided to run. 'Wow! It's flipping brilliant!' Soon, I'd really be achieving things with my running and in the background life would also take a turn for the better. Running is my salvation.

I see this with many of my clients - I meet a lot of people who are lost and who are using running as therapy. I have coached a number of clients to overcome alcohol addiction for example. I like to think they take a pint of my running enthusiasm which picks them up and points them in a new direction. I'm always super-busy which can be hard - it can feel like you have been drained of all your enthusiasm and have none left for yourself. Clients buy my time, and for those hours I'm theirs, totally theirs - for that period of time they get 100% of my running enthusiasm. So on a weekend off when it's my time to race and I know clients of mine will also be racing, I put on my headphones, tune in to some prog rock, and just go out there and lay it all on the line for myself. It's my time out, because life's busy and I need time on my own to play.

And because I feel such a profound need to run to salvage my soul, I actually think that when I get to marathon 1,000 it's going to be great, but it's not an Everest. It's going to have wow factor, but I'm not going to go, '998, 999, 1,000 - okay, done!' It's not like completing a 1,000-piece jigsaw because when I get there I'll just keep on going. No running feat will ever tick all of my boxes - running Everests won't lead me to salvation, it will make me feel content. It's the running itself that saves my soul.

# CHAPTER EIGHT

## LONDON TO LISBON

### LAID SO LOW - TEAR FOR FEARS 1992

*If you ever decide to run from London to Lisbon, you'll need this. It's Roland Orzabal at his best. Having chewed that bone far too low, I shed many tears listening to this over and over again on my 1,275-mile journey. Lyrically perfect in so many ways, it also showcases Orzabal's all-round musicianship including a great guitar solo. It's one of those tracks that unfortunately fades out and when the fade starts I hit replay.*

It would be unrealistic of me to pretend that every time I run a race, I run it hard. Some races are far from what I might describe as 'a brilliant Coleman performance!' Just like everyone else I have good and bad days, sometimes in the same race. Anyone that knows me will be familiar with the fact that I am not the biggest fan of running in the rain! I can think of a number of multi-day races I've done where I've started off really well for the first couple of days and then, yuk, it just hammers down with rain. I can remember races where it's rained so hard that I've had to shelter my eyes because the rain was actually hitting my eyeballs. Rain prohibits you from running well as you end up just ploughing rather than running and this in turn deflates your mood. Your whole mind-set changes and you just want to get to the finish, and get there as soon as possible so you can escape the weather. Then you finish, and maybe spend the night on a school hall or leisure centre floor surrounded by snoring runners so you can't get any sleep. At times like these you think, 'Why the heck am I doing this?'

I believe people worry too much about the present moment rather than looking forward and deducing that, 'Yes, things aren't great right now, but actually in a couple of hours I'll have showered and I'll be dry and warm and everything will be okay.' It's about seeing that bigger picture, isn't it? It's very much about treating running like it's a job. Maybe the fact that some of my running challenges have also doubled up as income streams has helped me to be more pragmatic and less emotional about the way I tackle races, particularly ultras or mega-day races.

With big challenges, I just say to myself, 'Well look, this running is what I'm doing for the next six hours or so today, get on with it. In many ways it's no different from a desk job - you go in, you get the job done and you go home.'

That's exactly how I approached London to Lisbon in 2004. On that trip we started at 09:00 every morning. This wasn't particularly early but by the time my crew and I had eaten breakfast and got ready we were rarely ready before then. It felt a bit like a foreign holiday because we were travelling through Europe, so we set aside time to enjoy it too with elevenses, lunch, afternoon tea, a late afternoon finish and finally dinner.

It was March 2004 when I'd originally received the call from 'Piranha Kid' - the PR company. They were part of 'Hill & Knowlton' which is one of the world's biggest advertising agencies. They'd pitched the idea to Gillette - one of their clients - who were launching the Right Guard Xtreme brand. The plan was to promote their new range of deodorant using an 'Extreme Fan'.

Following some quick calculations, I worked out that I only had a month to plan the run as it would take six weeks to reach Lisbon in time for the first game of Euro 2004. So it was very much crash, bang, wallop as far as the planning and organisation was concerned. No-one had made any attempt to start planning the run as they, 'didn't have a clue how to do it.'

My first job was to approach my boss at work. At the time I was working in the print game in London... 'I need six weeks of unpaid leave please!' They agreed and were in fact really supportive. For me, it was a double whammy as I was getting paid by the sponsor plus I got six weeks off work to go running. It couldn't be better, could it?

Next was to work out where the hell I was going. At the time we didn't have Google Maps or TomTom so I bought two Michelin Road Atlases (European Version) from WHSmith - one for me and one for my crew. I highlighted the route on both atlases - I would run along with the relevant page from one of them and in the motorhome my crew would follow the other. To supplement the atlas, both myself and my crew would have a simple Nokia mobile to simplify communication on the road.

Finally, I needed crew! I started looking for people as soon as I received that first call with little success and the agency was really struggling too. So, in desperation, I sent out a text message to all of my contacts which simply said, 'Does anybody want a six-week holiday to Portugal?' Two people replied saying they had friends who might be interested.

One was a lady called Sara who was a couple of years older than me and owned a café in London. So, if I'm being brutally honest, a part of me did think, 'Well, she'll be great because she can cook and she's a couple of years older than me which means she'll be a very matriarchal figure.' She was ideal - quite Bohemian and enjoyed a glass of red in the evening. She could also read a map which was brilliant.

The other was a fascinating guy who was about the same age as me called Sean. I soon discovered that he'd been at the Hillsborough Stadium at the time of the disaster and had been pronounced dead on the pitch. He'd subsequently been found still breathing and rushed off to Sheffield General. He met Princess Diana whilst still comatose, but promptly woke up when Liverpool's Manager, Kenny Dalglish, and some of the players visited, narrowly avoiding having his life support switched off. Typical Sean that.

Sean and I were kindred spirits as I'd been to a grammar school in Stratford-upon-Avon and he'd been to a grammar school in nearby Warwick. We consequently had a similar sense of humour and he turned out to be my 'partner in crime' for the entire journey.

Unfortunately, Sara and Sean didn't hit it off all the time. That said, as we travelled through some more remote parts of France and Spain where nobody spoke English, they depended on each other. For me, they were just extraordinary. They never once said, 'Can you get a move on?' or, 'You're being unreasonable.' They were the perfect supporters every step of the way - quite amazing given the first time I had met them was on the morning that we started the run. The three of us just looked at each other and thought, 'Okay, we're going to live with each other for the next six weeks, so let's get on with it.' It was gung-ho alright and made for a proper road-trip.

We hired this brand new giant motorhome which, after six weeks on the road, looked like it had been to Vietnam and back. It just got completely battered along the way. It stood out like a sore thumb on the challenge and attracted plenty of attention whenever we parked up.

One evening in France, we parked up in an empty town square only to discover we'd been completely boxed in when we awoke the next morning. For the purposes of the media campaign, I was 'England's Most Extreme Fan' so there was a giant St. George's Cross on the side of the motorhome. This is perhaps why, on another occasion, we woke up to discover it had been tagged with masses of French profanities!

A lot of room was taken up by countless pairs of running

shoes. My biggest fear was actually the camber of the road. Running into the oncoming traffic a few inches from the kerb is where the camber is the greatest. It puts a huge amount of pressure on your shins and can lead to a number of injuries, worst of which is the dreaded 'Anterior Compartment Syndrome' which can terminate any long distance run. Running in the UK was harder for me as I'm a heavy over-pronator with a shorter right leg. I therefore chose trainers with different ride heights - I actually ran in different styles and makes of trainer on each foot.

It was taking running to a kind of Formula 1 mentality - what with the telemetry your body feeds back over six weeks - you really tune in to how your body feels. You can almost feel every grain of grit on the road, every bit of tarmac underneath your feet. You get a real sense of touch for the surface you're running on. It was complete body telemetry and I felt completely tuned in.

As for the marathons I ran each day, they weren't the most taxing I've ever done... nor the speediest. I covered around 28 or 29 miles a day for 43 days. I was on the road for six weeks without a day off. There wasn't time for that. I ran my third marathon into Portsmouth Docks, crossed the Channel overnight and started the next marathon down the gangplank the next morning.

Running in France was totally different - it was so much more enjoyable than running from London to Portsmouth down the hard shoulder of the A3 dual carriageway for the first three days. Also, back in the UK people said, 'You can't park there,' or, 'You can't bring that thing in here.' In contrast, we could just park anywhere abroad - we stopped wherever I stopped that day. Some days there were local campsites, but a lot of the time we just stopped on the side of the road. Nobody ever questioned what we were doing. It banged home to me that, in the UK, there are a lot of 'jobsworths' and far too much red tape. The relaxed attitude in Europe proved most refreshing.

When I got to Portsmouth - I'd already done my 29 miles and told the ferry crew what I was doing. This somehow blagged me a trip up to the bridge - it was just fascinating being stood with the Captain watching the English Channel's busy traffic on these computer screens, and watching us navigate our way across to France. The screen summed up the entire challenge to a tee - every day felt like a new adventure with our own boats to circumnavigate and our own mini destination to reach.

We docked at St Malo. I'd been there when I was 12 on a school trip the weekend ABBA had won the Eurovision Song Contest. Here I was 30 years later, aged 42, going to the same place. Who'd have thought 30 years earlier that I'd be doing this? It was a great place to start the first of 25 days in France. What a huge country France was! It would be London to Portsmouth over eight times! And with that thought my French adventure began.

From St Malo, I ran mostly down the west coast, donning my UK's Most Extreme Fan get-up. The running was liberating as the crew didn't drive along behind me. I'd just say, 'The next town is 10km ahead - I'll see you there.' I just jogged along taking in the French countryside - it was so beautiful, especially if you veered off the beaten track. There was a real pattern to it, with town layouts being similar to those in the UK... a 'Welcome' sign into the town... a boulangerie, lots of pharmacists, a church, a pub, a tabac... and then an 'Exit' sign as you are leaving. A few more kilometres on, and there was another town exactly the same. France was like that all the way down to Bordeaux.

There was a wonderful ferry trip over the River Garonne at Royan and then from there all the way down to the Spanish border there were forests or, rather, one massive long forest road. Down it thundered trucks carrying huge logs, whistling past at 100kph. It was extremely dangerous. As I was running into the oncoming traffic, I eyeballed every single driver in every single car or truck so I could communicate my presence to them in the hope that they wouldn't hit me.

It seemed like millions of vehicles went by. I learned that the best ways to avoid becoming roadkill if a driver was getting a bit too close for comfort were to either wave at the driver or to stick your arm out at full length. If you stick out your arm, an oncoming car will miss you by about one metre - you tend to push the vehicle out into the road just that little bit more. Nonetheless, there were still occasions when it wasn't worth the gamble and I just thought, 'Okay, I'll move!' That was when I would dive for cover. But that was part of the adventure, wasn't it?

As with all big challenges I do, I started the challenge prepared for the worst - I'd put my house in order - made sure my bills were paid - just in case one of those cars hit me. And from thereon in, I spent the rest of the time looking for friendly faces to help me through my journey. Life at home continued whilst I was out on the road... My wife came to see me every two weeks which eased the pressure on me a bit in terms of my domestic life - she'd fly out for the weekend laden with litres of custard. In fact, everybody that visited me brought litres of custard because that was my main fuel... that and family sized quiches.

In extreme running terms, custard's great because it's just full of sugar. If you think about it, I was on the road for six weeks burning a huge amount of calories every day. Although the crew would go to French supermarkets, they just didn't have Ambrosia custard, and as soon as somebody said, 'There isn't any custard,' I just wanted it more. It's that thing about wanting what you can't have even more. As for the family sized quiches - they aren't normally known for their use as a sports supplement, but they were also fantastic. Their high calorie and fat dense consistency proved to be perfect and stopped me from losing too much weight. They kept me going quite nicely.

I'm now a qualified nutrition advisor and given the knowledge and experience I've gained since then, I'd approach the nutrition somewhat differently if a similar opportunity ever arose again - the protein shakes and recovery powders on the market today are excellent. But we're talking 2004 - that was more than ten years ago - nutrition has moved on leaps and bounds since then. Back then I just ate stodge and sugar with a tin of Coke mid-morning - I felt fantastic and was energised by whatever my crew could get their hands on.

Sara and Sean were brilliant. They cooked every day for me and as I approached the motorhome for my lunch, it would be served on a table with a tablecloth, laid with a knife and a fork. I'd just come in from the run and - bang - sit down, eat. It was really civilised. I ran with a little rucksack carrying a 2 litre Platypus, mobile 'phone, wallet and music player. It wasn't an iPod back then, just a regular Sony MP3 player, but it did the job. Tears for Fears accompanied me most of the way on that challenge!

London to Lisbon was a pilgrimage for me - that's how it felt. It was like a mental cleansing. I thought about everything - my kids, my job, what I was doing with my life.

I filmed a weekly video blog for 'Grandstand' and lots of radio stations 'phoned me asking where I was and why I was doing it. This helped to keep me going. The further I got, the better the story. As 'England's Most Extreme Fan', I was kitted out in England Football Kit for the trip and carried a huge St. George's Flag with 'Right Guard Xtreme' printed on it in huge letters. It was a great gig to follow the Flora 1,000 Mile Challenge with.

Every time I reached a big threshold - like going through 1,000 miles - it felt even better. BBC Radio Derby 'phoned me on their breakfast show at seven o'clock that morning saying, 'How is it going?' I nonchalantly replied, 'Well, I'm just about to go over the 1,000-mile line.' I tried to paint a picture for people back at home, I suppose, to try and explain what I was doing and why.

There were some really hairy moments along the way, especially when I entered Spain. I got lost in the middle of a place called Vitoria as my road maps just weren't detailed enough. There's a famous pilgrimage in Spain called Camino de Santiago de Compostela and, luckily for me, some of the pilgrims had congregated in the middle of the town square. To identify themselves, the pilgrims all donned a scallop shell emblem somewhere on their person. I approached a man with one such emblem on his rucksack with my only word of Spanish, 'Hola.' He replied in French... what a relief! So I reverted to my schoolboy French, 'Excusez-moi, monsieur. Est-ce que vous avez la carte?' To my delight, he pulled a complete road map of Vitoria out of his rucksack and pointed me in the right direction. So I left the city and was reunited with my crew.

There were a number of moments like that where you just thought, 'I'm not quite sure how that happened.' Maybe it was also a spiritual journey for me... with the millions of cars coming at me from the other direction, it felt like I was being looked down on from above. Going into some of the towns along the way, there were lots of shrines and crosses and all sorts of religious effects, and I certainly did feel on many occasions that there was a nice, friendly, warm hand on my back looking after me.

It was certainly dangerous being out there on your own but somehow the euphoria of the challenge outweighed any fears or negativity I might otherwise have felt.

Nonetheless, some things were a real nuisance!

One Sunday morning, for example, I was talking to my wife on my mobile and she was asking me how to operate the motor mower because she wanted to mow the lawn at home. She was, quite rightly, bending my ear about the grass being a foot long. You get into one of those conversations, don't you?

I was saying, 'Well, I'm really sorry,' whilst trying to explain to this tiny woman how to use one of the pull starters on a mower! It just wouldn't start.

To explain further, I stopped and put my rucksack down on the floor... and my back went. I'd pulled a ligament or something. Now I wasn't happy either. Who cares about the bloody mower - my back had gone and I still had a good 15 days to go. For the next four days it was agony. I walked like John Inman - like a velociraptor - I had to move really gingerly to protect my back but still had to cover the miles.

So with the wheels well and truly off, I was thinking, 'What on earth am I going to do?' My thoughts were to just keep on going. It was less than 30 miles a day - I could walk that. I later found out it was a disc herniation in my lower back which could have been a real deal-breaker for the challenge - I'd ruptured it when I was in my twenties lifting furniture. Back then I'd gone to a physio who had given me some exercises that had really helped. So I looked for a safe, flat place where I could do them and hopefully feel some relief.

Luckily I found some grass, so I started press-upping away on the floor only to look up and find I was surrounded by four huge German Shepherd dogs. In that one moment, I relived a terrible dog incident from when I was four, as well as all my dog fears from The Desert Cup.

Even worse, they were all gnashing their teeth. Within a millisecond I picked up my belongings and ran. I ran like a 400 metre runner away from the devil, thinking, 'Do you know what? My back's not really that bad? Stop dicking about and just get on with the running.' Talk about instant relief... I'm not kidding, I just carried on without any further back pain.

The beauty of going on a journey from A to B is the constant change of scenery - it's a sensory overload, 'Oh, look at this! Look at that!' Some of the places in Spain were truly unique. Have you been to Valladolid in Central Spain? It's breath-taking as were so many other places that we passed through. Many of them were off the beaten track so it felt like a real voyage of discovery, and the locals were incredibly kind to me and the crew. When you run 161 laps of Mick's Barry 40, the senses are somewhat dimmed with the repetition - you become very introspective. In contrast, my run to Lisbon was a constant feast of new experiences - so much so that I decided to start writing my blog. Every day I'd write about something I'd seen on the road or something that had happened. I took photos and just saw some amazing places - it was such a fascinating journey.

And there were some really funny things that happened. On one occasion, my mobile rang and it was Sara. I was thinking, 'Oh dear, what's happened?' I answered, saying, 'I can't hear you because there's an old plane flying low above me.' And she replied, 'I know, I'm in it!'

'What do you mean you're in the plane?'

She said, 'I went out for a bicycle ride waiting for you to come along and I met Gilles. Gilles asked me if I would like a go in his plane!'

It was just one of many bizarre moments.

There was also a magical sense of naivety about the challenge. I remember vividly on one of the days some way in I could barely run, and I was running along the hard shoulder thinking, 'Bloody hell - this is hard work. I guess I must be pretty fatigued by now.' Then I discovered that I was actually in the Pyrenees and hadn't even noticed the climb into the mountains! Pretty ridiculous really but that was part of it. It was spontaneous.

Every time my running crossed over the page in the atlas - and I'm talking a normal, standard-sized car atlas - we tore it off and stuck it on the outside of the toilet wall in the camper van. We gradually began to form a giant map of Europe - it might take two or three days to complete a page, but as the map grew we began to see the enormity of the run. Distance-wise, it was a twentieth of the world's circumference. And I did it just using my two feet!

My story really kicked in when I reached the border with Portugal. The Portuguese media had really bought into the fact that somebody had run all the way from London to come to their Euro finals. I was greeted at the Spain-Portugal border by the Lady Mayor of Marvão - a very ancient city which is a World Heritage site at the top of some beautiful mountains. It was an extraordinary place to visit and I was instantly made a Freeman of the city! I really must go back one day thinking about it. It wasn't all good news though - the media had feedback from the Euro 2004 organisers in Lisbon... 'You can't arrive on match day because of the security around the ground. You'll have to arrive a day earlier.'

So, instead of finishing off with a nice easy 30 miles a day for the last four days, I now had to do 40 miles a day for three. It meant getting up earlier to run the extra miles and wasn't ideal at the end of six weeks of running.

That said, when I'd seen the first road sign for Portugal it felt amazing! It felt like I'd been on the road forever so it was such a relief to finally reach Portugal. It was then that I allowed myself to start a final countdown.

I followed the most direct route which meant running through farmlands and down tiny roads for miles before finally descending into Lisbon. That was when I caught sight of the corner of the stadium that I'd been running towards for six weeks. It just popped into sight for a second between some houses... and that's when my knees buckled. That was a real life moment. Even now, thinking about it sends shivers down my spine. It felt like I'd scored a goal in the final itself. It was just a fabulous moment. After six weeks of running, the journey really had a meaning.

I didn't know much about football, quite ironic given I was 'England's Most Extreme Fan' - England's least informed fan more like! Nonetheless, I was really looking forward to the game. Unfortunately France won 2-1, so I'd run 1,275 miles to watch England lose!

The real irony, however, was that although it took me six weeks to get there, it only took five and a half hours to fly home. It was a truly life-changing experience - I believed I'd found 'heaven' on the way. You get to the end of something like that and you feel complete inner calm: you've processed everything along the way; you've got to the stage where you've thought about everything that you could possibly have thought about. It was a cleansing process and maybe at the time I had thought that this was going to be the last chapter in the book.

Not so surprising, perhaps, when you consider professional sportspeople are referred to as 'veterans' at the age of 40 these days. I had run 500 marathons by that point and I was 42 - a veteran runner. So maybe my book was complete? At the time, London to Lisbon really did feel like the ultimate trip.

Crucially, my London to Lisbon road trip made me an authority on running which has helped me enormously in my coaching career. I was talking to a client recently about his endless battle with blisters, and I said, 'Well, you wear your socks inside out.' He just looked at me like my lights had gone out but that's something I learnt going to Lisbon. If you turn your socks inside out you put all the seams of the socks on the outside rather than next to your feet. It's simple, really, as the seams no longer rub against your feet. In fact socks only lasted a day - I simply had to throw them away. Socks and sun cream got eaten up, just like the custard.

I also learnt a tremendous amount about shoe technology whilst out pounding all that tarmac... which shoes worked and how long they worked for. You can't run day after day after day on tarmac in the same shoes. You have to alternate different styles of shoe that put different pressures on different bones in your feet. On reflection there were only certain brands/types of trainers that would have worked for my road trip but I had to work that out for myself as I was breaking boundaries in running back in 2004. There was nobody to help me discover which shoes would work, so I just experimented with lots of brands and styles by simple trial and error. Once I'd figured out which ones worked and why, I stuck to them. I actually ran to Lisbon in Saucony trainers which were fantastic - I wouldn't have got there without them.

Nowadays, when I buy a new pair of trainers there are certain pieces that I cut straight out - I learnt that going to Lisbon too. Inevitably trainer manufacturers haven't tested their shoes to the same extent as me! As a result of all this road testing I've been really lucky - I've been running injury-free since the day I started.

On reflection, there were other bigger challenges I wish I had done on my return. Running The London Marathon every day for a year, starting and finishing with the race itself, was certainly up there. It would have been a really fascinating thing to do and something that Joe Public could easily relate to: it's probably the most famous marathon in the world and it's in the UK. One thing I had learned from London to Lisbon was that, as soon as your running adventure takes you overseas, the British media interest drops and you're out of people's hearts and minds. I'm a bit of a media whore - I thrive in the spotlight and want to please my peers - completing a British challenge on the world's most famous marathon course would have been just awesome... you'd be able to collate a fantastic set of photos running down the same streets in all the different climates and conditions. It would have made a great YouTube movie, wouldn't it? That's the kind of thing that really fires me up.

In fact for me, the real highpoints during London to Lisbon were the bits where I was talking on TV, the bits where I was connecting with people back at home with the blog - those bits were really great. My blog in those days was very different - I just used to write an A4 document and send it to people's email addresses as there was no blogging website and no Facebook.

If I were to replicate the event now it would be much bigger news. I'd be tweeting all day long and facebooking pictures every few miles - people would almost be able to accompany me on my journey. In 2004, the day-to-day grind was almost private. It didn't really get the publicity that it should have got - there were masses of pictures in The Star and The Sun but it wasn't big news in the broadsheets.

The media also helped to keep me focused on the task in hand - from the outset I knew that my contacts at 'BBC Breakfast' and 'Grandstand' would be waiting for me at the finish. So, for me, the finish line was going to be my party - my Christmas that year. I was greeted by the Lady Ambassador of Lisbon, Rob Bonnet from BBC Breakfast and BBC 5 Live. Rob Bonnet took me away immediately to the rooftop BBC Studio in Lisbon where we did an interview - I loved it. It's that Show Pony in me isn't it? It's that bit where I say, 'Ta Da! Look at what I've just achieved! This is my story!'

Why such a grand turnout? Because you've got the second biggest football tournament in the world, it's the day before the championship starts, and all the world's press are there with nothing to report home about except this crazy bloke who's run all the way from England. It was brilliant!

I've got photographs of me arriving at the finish there - I waved flagpoles with both of my both hands and I reckon I danced the last mile. I just felt so fit and so elated to finish. I was lean - I'd probably lost perhaps a couple of stone on the way so I was tiny except for my giant calf muscles that were bigger than my quads after six weeks on the road.

If I was only allowed to do one running challenge ever, this would be my choice. It was just so massive: surviving 43 days on the road... running every day uninjured... using all the skills I'd built up over the years... testing my mental toughness... testing my body to find out just how hard my body was... seeing if I could cope and if I could find my way through it. It was the ultimate test at that time.

The way if affected me afterwards, however, was odd. It was a bit like completing a jigsaw - you can't wait to finish the puzzle, but when the puzzle is finished, the bubble bursts. I hit the world back home with an almighty bump - the challenge had a far more profound and lasting effect on my life than I could ever have anticipated.

Two people had supported me all that way - I felt very humbled when I had time to reflect and realise that, without them, I wouldn't have got there. I felt a huge sense of gratitude towards them. What's more, I learnt a lot about my personal tolerance levels on that run and that I'm somebody who doesn't really ask for much help from people. I don't really talk to other people about my feelings. Why? I'm very old school with the way I handle things. In my opinion, admitting to your shortcomings weakens your resolve meaning it's very difficult to complete life challenges such as London to Lisbon.

So I'll never really say that I'm tired or feeling fatigued or ache or hurt when I'm running because you can't be like that if you want to survive. You have to make your mind and attitude gladiatorial.

This attitude spills over into my everyday non-running life. I like to think I am a very positive person - sometimes it can be hard to sustain when I'm training people every day. Sometimes you feel like you've had all your life-blood sucked out of you. I think that's because running for many people is like an exorcism of their inner demons, and in a way I act as their priest. After all, when people go to church they don't give a second thought to the spiritual needs of the vicar, do they? When does a vicar go to church? He doesn't, because he's meant to be there at the front telling the congregation all about God and how good it is to be a Christian. So how does he get to fulfil his spiritual needs?

Lisbon certainly fed me spiritually - maybe I undertook the challenge at a time when I was searching for something else. Maybe I'd gotten to the end of the running road? When I returned from my run, had I found what I was looking for? Actually, after 1,275 miles I concluded that, no, I hadn't. Rather than London to Lisbon being my swansong, I realised that running was now an integral part of my life and a very important part of who I'd become. After all, David Gilmour of Pink Floyd didn't stop playing the guitar once their final album had been released. It didn't matter that they weren't recording any new albums - he still carried on playing... and that was the same with my running. I didn't want to just forget it, buy a motorbike or sports car, and never give running a second thought. Running was my therapy, and London to Lisbon had just been an exceptionally good session with the shrink.

# CHAPTER NINE

## CAREER CHANGE

### PENDULUM - 9000 MILES 2008

*I'll admit I'm a late convert to the Aussie Drum and Bass Duo but I bought all three studio albums in quick succession. It's loud, fast, melodic and really, really clever stuff. Robert Swire-Thompson is such a great Lead-Singer/Producer and there are some amazing live Glastonbury performances on YouTube that are well worth a look. The bass rattles my walls at home and really makes the sub come to life. It's music that makes you feel as though you've known it all your life yet it's still completely fresh. It's great running music and you will soon get the feel of the 'Pendulum' kicking in when each track gets going.*

No matter what people tell you, you'll need to find your own version of what works best for you, be it in running, work or everyday life. Play to your own strengths, not to someone else's. Take Black Friday for example, that newly imported fad from the States where everyone's supposed to get whipped up into a frenzy because some supermarkets are offering discounted products. What a load of old tosh - but there we go. It's amazing how people get themselves drawn into it! It just highlights the fact that the world is full of sheep. Go your own way I say - that's what I do. Some weeks I run up to four marathons. I run them with clients as part of their MdS training and I get paid to do them. You don't need to wait for permission to go for a long run and an adventure. Just get out there like I do and make it happen.

Of course that's not to say I always jump out of bed, bursting to go for a run. Actually on quite a few days, just like everyone else, I think, 'Can I be arsed?' But it's my job, isn't it? And I just think how awful it would be to be stuck in an office. It's interesting to find out what my clients do for a living - it helps me to understand their personality and get a feel for what makes them tick...

For example, I remember a lady coming to see me who's a lawyer - she gets paid to work 35 hours a week but works double that amount. She earns £80k a year and just accepts that, 'That's the job and I need to be seen to be putting in the hours.' In my opinion she's more like a registered charity giving her company £40k a year of work for nothing. She's bonkers!

I'm 54 now, not 34, and at 34 you have different work aspirations, don't you? It's only as you get older that you realise you've been miss-sold the lie that you must kill yourself at work to get ahead. Many of my clients are stuck on the work-life treadmill - they work long hours to earn their large salaries which finance their expensive lifestyles. They are stuck in a rut. In actual fact, for how many of these working hours are they honestly productive and earning their salary? Most folk I meet respond to emails in an instant and spend a lot of their days on Facebook or YouTube watching other people doing things that they really want to be doing themselves.

I think a lot of people spend a significant proportion of their working hours responding to personal emails, sorting out their finances and wasting time talking to colleagues. I can't understand companies that let their staff go outside to smoke cigarettes during their working day.

For me personally, I got to the stage where I thought, 'Well, I'm earning myself X, but I'm actually earning the company Y.

Why am I earning somebody else's fortune for them?' When I returned from Lisbon I felt like I had retired from running. How could it get any bigger or better? So I just went back to work. Eventually, I just couldn't be the corporate person they wanted me to be any more, sucking up to clients and towing the party line, maintaining professional but rather artificial 'friendships' with the clients you believed would sign your contracts. Ironically, I was actually very successful at it and my sales figures were high, but it wasn't the type of life I wanted to lead.

By 2005 I was losing my mojo - work wasn't fun and neither was running. Psychologically, I was in the doldrums. 2005 to 2007 were my leanest marathon years ever. I did 25 marathons in 2005, 24 in 2006 and 22 in 2007. Training-wise I did very little - very little indeed. I'd take weeks off - I just stopped. I felt like I was becoming quite bland. Maybe I was becoming… normal! That was my biggest fear.

Towards the end of 2005 I thought to myself, 'What the hell is going on?' I tried to get a bit of the magic back by entering the Marathon des Sables in 2006. I hadn't done it for six years and my hope was that, by doing it, the skies would suddenly turn blue, the grass would turn green and the little white fluffy bunnies would be running around in the fields again! But, 'Oh my God!' The organisers had made it so much harder… LOADS harder.

When I returned from Morocco I started to cherry-pick my races rather than just run every race I could. One of them was a race in Chile called 'The Atacama Crossing'. It's the same format as the MdS but at high-altitude in the Atacama Desert. With the exception of the Antarctic it's the driest place on Earth - it hasn't rained there for 400 years. Barclaycard paid for me to be part of their three-man team that year so I enjoyed an all-expenses trip! What could be better?

Unlike the MdS which has helicopters, doctors and well

established communications, the Atacama Crossing is completely stripped bare. If you hurt yourself seriously out there it's far more dangerous, even life-threatening. There's nothing there! Honestly, nothing at all. You can't drive a 4x4 from one end of the course to the other - it traverses mountains high in the Andes. It's where they tested the lunar rover for the space moon landings in my youth so I had a great interest in seeing where this had actually taken place. It's absolutely stunning - a totally different kind of desert from the Sahara. There was an active volcano erupting on the horizon! It's the most extraordinary place ever and I felt really privileged to be there even though the event was totally scary. During the day it was 25°C, at night it was a bitterly cold -15°C - I nearly froze to death every night!

Each day we'd run for at least eight hours. On the long day we camped out - I think we were out there for well over 24 hours. Thankfully, all my MdS skills came in handy but the race wasn't so compassionate to my companions Douglas and Tommo. Tommo's feet - he trashed those very early on and by the end he had no skin on his heels at all. I had decided to do the race in fancy dress with my flag and I actually pulled him along for two days with the flagpole. He just held onto it and ran/walked behind.

We did it as a team, so we actually had to go through all the checkpoints together. At one particular checkpoint it turned out that Douglas' feet weren't much better. We stopped for half an hour - I just sat down while they got their feet patched up and then we were off again.

The camaraderie was fantastic. Douglas told us the whole Shackleton story one night whilst we plodded along in the dark. Shackleton's ill-fated trip seemed quite apt taking our situation into account. It took him about an hour and a half to tell us the story - and at the end of it we just said, 'Can you tell us again?' So he did.

With both the MdS 2006 and the Atacama Crossing under

my belt, I really started to ponder my future. I decided I was going to forget about the smaller races and focus on BIG stuff because these were the types of events that attracted media and publicity which is what I really enjoyed.

The other thing I started to realise was that, actually, maybe this wasn't all about me. My wife at the time said to me, 'Look, you're always teaching people how to run. Why don't you take a career break from what you're doing at the moment and get an official qualification that means you can teach people how to run professionally?' Up until this point running had only existed in my 'solo world'. I spent many many years learning about running and I didn't share my experiences with anyone until 2006 because it was my private little world that I didn't want to be invaded. It was only in 2006 that I worked out I could make a living out of my intellectual property…

… And it wasn't until 2008 that I bit the bullet and signed up for a Personal Training Diploma with Lifetime Fitness - it felt like I was going back to school with lots of 19 year olds. I asked them how long it took to complete the course and I was told 18 months to two years. But by my reckoning, if I doubled up on the modules and did two or even three exams a week, I could actually do it in 14 weeks.

Until then I'd never lifted weights, in fact I'd never even set foot in a gym! Within 14 weeks I had passed 16 modules and been awarded my Personal Training Diploma - I was really proud of myself. More importantly, I had a new spring in my step as I had now worked out how to use what I'd learnt over the last 20 years of running to help other people.

It was a complete role reversal thinking about it. Until then I'd spent all of my life in different areas of the print and design business, building the name and reputation of each business I worked for. This was a process that involved a significant amount of, 'Look at me! Look at me! Look at me!' Now I've ended up being a teacher.

When I signed up with Lifetime Fitness, I asked them, 'What can I do to improve my skills while I'm doing this Personal Training Diploma?' And they said, 'Why don't you get fit?' In days gone by I would have been tempted to say, 'Do you know who I am?' But I took it on the chin and thought, 'Do you know what? Maybe I should get really fit again.' It was time to reassess my standards and raise the bar again.

I restarted training, this time using the new skills I'd learnt in the gym... I started lifting weights, exercising my core and adding some proper periodization. I felt exceptionally fit and lean - I did the MdS again in 2009 and achieved my best ever result out there. Why? Because I'd run a lot of miles - loads and loads of miles. I would run for hours on treadmills, I completed hours of the now legendary Coleman Power Hours and, psychologically, my running confidence had returned. On a personal note I was finally back on track.

Professionally, however, I still had some big issues to overcome. In my first month of personal training I earned £180. I'm not kidding - it was hideous. My ego took a real hit. I thought at the time, 'What the f*** am I doing?' I was based at a Fitness First gym in the centre of Derby and there weren't a great deal of punters that I could entice into running back-to-back marathons for 40 days... none in fact! All the men wanted to bulk up and all the women were desperate to be thin.

For all that I enthused about marathon-running, I may as well have been speaking Russian, and if your job is paying the mortgage you can't do many £180 months before it all goes a bit 'Pete Tong', can you? But do you know what? It really taught me how to speak to people, how to connect with them, how to get people to see where I was coming from. The Internet also became my friend - I thought, 'Well, I've got to have a USP. I've got to have something that sets me aside from all the other personal trainers in the UK. What have I got? I've got nine world records, I've done the MdS, I'd run several hundred marathons.

That makes me a number one, super-elite. That takes me to the top of the pyramid. I wanted to be the 'go-to' expert for people who wanted to do similar running challenges to the ones I'd completed. I could teach them everything they needed to know as I had first-hand knowledge... and lots of it... so I could fast-track them to success.

Then I thought about the Marathon des Sables - that could be my biggest seller! I built a website and completely rebranded myself - it was a complete reincarnation. So there I was starting again at 46 having to muddle through financially and putting a lot of effort back into my running. In fact all of the gaps in between the not-many-clients I had were spent running on treadmills. I built up my fitness as I thought, 'Well, if you're going to take on a huge challenge, you've got to be fit. You've got to live the dream.'

I picked up quite a few clients whilst I was at the MdS in 2009. In 2010 and 2011 it just exploded! But 2009, that was when I realised that I wasn't just there for the run, I was also there for the hustle. It was a business trip as much as a pleasure trip and it still is.

It marked a real turning point in the way I approached my working life. If you're working for somebody else, quite often there isn't an awful lot of incentive to go the extra mile and excel at what you're doing. Getting the job done is enough - your salary gets paid at the end of each month and that's it - thanks very much. If you're working for yourself, though, well then it really matters.

These days there aren't enough hours in the day. I talk about the MdS to people every single day of my life - every day, because people are fascinated by it. It's the Manchester United of ultra races - it's got that Manchester United branding in the running world. To date, I've done it 13 times and coach over a hundred people each year to run it. My clients appreciate my no nonsense approach to the MdS and to the training because I've got nothing to prove - I just tell it as it is. They travel from all over the world to see me and hear the facts about the race one-to-one.

Making the decision to work for myself was tough - you don't know whether it's going to succeed and you have to give it time. It's not a three-month project. It's not a six-month project, really - it's an ongoing situation you have to constantly reassess.

Even now, at 54, I have to think to myself - well, in ten years' time, can I still run four marathons a week with people? Can I still - at 64 - relate to 24 year olds the way I do now? I'm meeting people who are the same age as my kids. I can relate to them because they're just like my kids. But by the time I'm 64, will I have to reinvent myself again? I'll have to be a different person to the one I am now so that I can still make my living.

Thankfully my reputation has built up to such an extent now that, these days, I don't necessarily have to physically run marathons with people, even though I do still find it therapeutic for myself. I've become a kind of fitness life coach and get a great amount of pleasure from it. I now work from home every day - I have done since I completed my Diploma in 2008. Nonetheless I obviously spend a large amount of time out of the house with clients - be it accompanying them on marathons, coaching them at the gym, pushing them to sprint up hills or taking them to the local running shop to make sure they buy the right trainers.

I've put a lot of work into becoming the 'go-to' coach for everything from 12 week training plans to crushing alcohol addiction. As my new career gained momentum I neglected other parts of my life - my marriage clashed with both work and running. Work and running - my God - those two things are hand-in-hand for me now and I've publicly blogged about my life story for years.

Have I achieved all of my running desires and aspirations yet? I need to think about that. I've certainly built up the fitness brand I was hoping for. I don't know if I ever envisaged it being the David Lloyd of fitness centres, but if you type 'Marathon des Sables training' into Google, my name comes up. In fact, if you type anything ultramarathon-related into Google my name comes up, I'm there. I love being the authority on things, so coaching has actually put me in a position whereby I'm advising my peers rather than seeking to please them.

One of the perks of becoming recognised as the 'go-to' expert for all things ultra is that I've been lucky enough to coach a number of celebrity clients. I've coached many household names to run the MdS including Sir Ranulph Fiennes, Mark Lewis-Jones [Game of Thrones; Star Wars], Richard Harrington [Hinterland] and Tom Aikens [celebrity chef]. I've also coached Blue Peter's presenter Helen Skelton to run the Namibian 24 Hour Desert Ultra.

In fact I enjoy loads more PR and publicity by working with celebrities than I ever would on my own because outside of the running world, people just go, 'Who the hell is Rory Coleman?' Working with celebrities has opened up a whole new world to me.

I trained Helen, the 'Blue Peter' girl, in 2009 and earned my Blue Peter badge at the age of 48. I was on the BBC books for thirteen weeks and got paid by the BBC as a contributor. The Namibian 24 Hour Desert Ultra was her challenge of choice which entailed running 78 miles in 24 hours across the Namib Desert. I coached her for 76 days. When we started, she was a 2.5-hour half-marathon runner and a running novice. She was fantastic - such a lovely person - what you see is what you get. She just said, 'Rory, tell me what to do and I'll do it.' So we worked really, really hard for 76 days and she actually finished eighth in the race.

We made sure she did something on each and every one of those 76 days to improve her chances of doing well at the race. So she was in the gym, she was running miles. Of course she had filming commitments, but we worked around all of those. Her parents live in the Lake District so we ran a couple of back-to-back marathons there. She ran 30 miles around Carlisle Football Ground one day. We went to Marrakech and ran a marathon together. We ran a marathon in London together. It was fantastic working with her - she was so much fun. Everywhere we went people knew who she was - Blue Peter is held with such reverence as we have all grown up with Blue Peter - it's a British institution!

From a work perspective, it also gave me a lot more exposure to people outside of my target market. I now appealed to a much wider audience. Okay, it's a kids' audience, but lots of other people watch that show too. Next, Facebook and Twitter began to kick in and both were tools that I could also use to drive my brand forwards. And then there's this book! Every good coach or ultra-runner has a book don't they?! People seem to be fascinated by what drives ultra-runners to do such extreme challenges. Well, here I am...

Marketing and publicity wasn't something that I cottoned onto immediately. It took me a long time to realise its importance, particularly since I'm not a reader myself. I eventually took the plunge to embark on this book following countless prompts from clients. You really are a 'nobody', it seems, unless you have written a book! People want to know what makes you tick... they also want to take you apart word by word!

People seem to live in a self-imposed 'comfort zone' - they hate being taken outside of it and end up playing it a bit safe most of the time. This is why the book is so important - it provides escapism - it allows people to read about incredible adventures and feats and let their imaginations run away with them. And ironically that was me in 2006 - I started playing it safe, started taking it easy, thinking, 'Oh well, I've done it - I've done the marathons. I've been to the Atacama - that was alright. It was scary, but I came back alive.'

In Northern Ireland they say, 'How are you doing?'

And people reply, 'I'm sticking out.'

'How're you doin'?'

'Stickin' out.'

I didn't want to 'Stick out' anymore. What could I do next?

Well, actually, this - my new coaching venture. I've been doing it for eight years now and it's by far the best job I've ever had. I determine when I work - I determine what people do when they come to see me. I open my front door to new people every day and I never know what I'm going to get. It's up to me to coach and entertain that person as they are my guest, and I have to quickly understand what they're all about.

It's not about me, it's about them, and I'm working out their personality traits - what makes them tick, what doesn't make them tick - and trying to realign their lives just like I did 20 years ago. I make people believe they are extraordinary rather than plain ordinary. I'm not ordinary - I believe I'm extraordinary. Actually, I believe we are all extraordinary but by conforming to society's ideals we become bland. It's like being coated with a layer of magnolia paint, but when you peel back the magnolia you find a Mona Lisa lurking underneath.

So I needed to find somebody that did what I did, and that's what happened. It started with a very brief conversation between me and my wife now, Jenny, on the last day of the MdS 2009. Something just sparked.

Back in '99, the MdS had changed my life - I'd left my wife and my job and got away from it for a few years before re-orbiting to meet my third wife. The race had re-fired my running in 2006 only to destroy my marriage in 2009. I finally found somebody that understood me - that actually got that it was okay to stick out and just said, 'I do this stuff too - I know how you feel. I know how this makes you feel.' And also she's at the top of the pyramid as a runner. She's the best, literally, and finished top British female runner at the MdS 2009-12. She was also the National 100km Champion in 2014 and has represented Team GB at 24 hour racing.

I told her how bad her trainers were. It was the morning of the last day of the race and I just said, 'How are you doing?' You just get talking to people at these events, don't you? And she said, 'My feet are killing me!' so I replied, 'Well, you're wearing the wrong trainers.' Did I know what I was doing? Probably. Was I trying it on? Well, you know me, I'm an old charmer.

When we came back to the UK, we just got chatting about running - there just seemed to be a connection. For the next 18 months we spoke a lot, and when you start talking to somebody that understands you, you start to look forward to talking to them, they understand how you feel, and so on. Then in 2010 we became a couple.

It must be hard for people to live with me unless they understand me and my world. I'm not somebody that would tell you about the inner depths of my soul too easily, unless I'm confessing all in a book like this of course. I don't tend to share my really dark stuff with the person I live with, probably because I see it as a weakness... I'm pretty old school. I am getting better at it, but a lot of the time I just don't want to discuss things as they're history. I'm not interested in the past - it's all about the future for me. I love anticipating what's next - that's what makes me tick.

I think I've done that phase of clocking a mass of running achievements, like my Guinness World Records. Now I'm in the 'building my epitaph' phase, doing stuff that people are going to remember me for.

Look at Sir Ranulph Fiennes. He's got his books, he's got his book tour, he does his talking - he has a whale of a time going and speaking to people. I did an event with him - the guy's mobbed everywhere he goes - people instantly know who he is and it's almost like they want to touch the cloak to get healed. They want to drink in Sir Ranulph Fiennes! I'd love that! I am constantly surprised at how many people new to ultra-running have heard of me, and I have started to get 'papp'd' whilst out running, particularly down at our local sand dunes, so perhaps I'm getting there!

So cutting back to 2010 and 2011, with Jenny by my side, I decided to really focus on coaching other people. Jenny was also keen to build her running cv so we did lots of things with her. I started to work out how I could help her become even more formidable at running - she wanted to set the world record for the fastest crossing of Ireland from Malin Head at the top to Mizen Head at the bottom. So we went over there and she beat the existing world record, set by a man, by over 15 hours. I felt a real part of that record as I gave her a massive amount of support and she had all my knowledge at her fingertips to tap into.

I was the nice cop, nasty cop sometimes. You've got to be both - you've got to be loving, you've got to be firm, you've got to be questioning, you've got to be supportive but most of all you've got to be protective. You have to be all of those things. On top of that she obviously had the great ability to carry it off, but I felt like I could enjoy and even accept a small part of the glory when we watched her crossing the finish line at Mizen Head. For me, it was almost like, 'Look at what I've helped to create.'

Our relationship is a bit like Gary Locke and world marathon best holder Paula Radcliffe. Gary was a really good runner but Paula - she's the best athlete that the UK has ever produced.

Well, there's Jenny - she's a GB triathlete, indoor rowing champion, and she's one of those people that is just really good at everything. So I have shared her glory with her. And the interesting thing is, because I was training her to get better and better and better, she actually started to coach me. She turned the tables a bit.

I think, because there are 13 years between us, I was always a little bit self-deprecating, blaming it on my age, saying I was this 'old codger'. But she would say, 'No, you're not an old codger and you could go a lot faster than you do.' So she very subtly started pushing the buttons, saying, 'Come on... start speeding up.' And it really worked. I did some races and started winning my age category. I did some marathons and started getting nearer to my old PBs again. And it's just fuelled my fire to do more!

# CHAPTER TEN

## 28 MARATHONS IN 28 DAYS

SHAKING THE TREE (LIVE) - PETER GABRIEL 1989

*A second track for Sir Peter of Gabriel and why not? This live version is very different to the original with Youssou N'Dour and benefits greatly from the additional vocals of Paula Cole. The band includes Tony Levin on bass and David Rhodes on lead guitar as well as Manu Katche on drums. They play so tightly together that the whole 'Secret World' album is a total triumph and is in fact my favourite live album. There's a great video of the album too that's well worth a view.*

I recently went to see Peter Gabriel live in concert at the Motorpoint Arena in Cardiff. It was an experience that put my entire life and running career into perspective. The last time I had seen him was at the Hammersmith Odeon in 1978 and it was quite an epiphany.

His music is an integral part of my life. He's one of my all-time heroes and there he was, just a few feet in front of me. Back in 1978 he'd actually come out into the audience and I'd shaken his hand. But I hadn't seen him for 36 years! All that life of mine and his had just vaporised in that time and this journey that I've been on, this massive journey I've experienced since the last time I saw him in concert… wow it really hit home!

I looked at him and I just thought, 'My God! He's 65!' When

I saw him last he would have been a young guy, much younger than I am now. It just shows you that life goes by in a click of your fingers. That said, I also thought, 'Even at 65, he's still just got IT. The guy's just got that amazing 'X' Factor.' He has a brilliant way with people and audiences and when he sings, he's incredible. He didn't learn this stuff overnight - he's had a long career in music - all that experience and sheer professionalism, I find it so inspiring. I think he's become a different person through the years - his music's changed and he's mellowed, definitely.

He was at his peak with Genesis in 1974 and 1975. Then he just decided, 'Do you know what? I don't want to do it anymore. I want to go out and do something else.' And maybe that's a trait we share - maybe that's a trait of Aquarian men if you believe in astrology - his birthday is a week after mine. We're a bit strange us Aquarians - we don't like being told what to do and, sometimes, we do just walk away from stuff because we've done it. Why continue to do something when you inherently know that it's not right for you?

Conversely, you meet many people who persistently pursue a business ideal that is fated from day one - they make themselves bankrupt in the process working all of the hours God sends when it is clear as crystal to onlookers that it is destined for failure from the outset. Take 'Dragon's Den' for example - people appear on that programme who've invested hundreds of thousands of pounds into ideas that will never be the big money spinners they believe them to be. More often than not, within ten seconds flat one of the Dragons just says, 'That idea's rubbish. Go away and stop wasting all of our time and money.'

There's a tendency to keep thrashing away at things when actually it's okay to say, 'Do you know what? I've failed. I'll go and do something else.' Maybe the thing you're pursuing isn't ticking all of those boxes that you need ticking. You gradually get sucked in and end up getting forced down more and more avenues that you don't want to go down. Then eventually something happens and you just snap and go against it, you make a decision to walk away from it. I sometimes find myself in that predicament too - I find failure extremely hard to swallow so have a tendency to keep working at things long after I should have put my hands up and walked away. That was why I turned to booze in the past.

The opportunity to run Stoptober came along at the end of a 20-year period of running and of personal ups and downs - it seemed like a fitting climax to those two decades as 20 years is a huge amount of time. Public Health England approached me to see if I would be interested in helping them to publicise their non-smoking campaign. Their remit was to encourage more than 250,000 people in the UK to give up smoking and there I was, an ex 40-a-day smoker, being the inspirational focus of their media campaign. All those years ago I would have said, 'Don't be daft! I'm a hardened smoker. I'm a 40-a-day man, and I'm certainly not going to travel around the UK telling people to quit smoking.' How the tables had turned! I felt very fortunate and proud to be asked. These opportunities do seem to just land on my doorstep - I'm very fortunate in that way. My family would say that my bread would always land butter-side up. I'm one of those people.

It all started with an email I received from a PR company in London who were working with Public Health England at the time. The idea was that if you can quit smoking for 28 days, you're five times more likely to give up smoking for good. They were planning 15 roadshows in cities across the UK which had a high prevalence of smoking. The destinations included Bristol, Newcastle, Reading and Stoke-on-Trent, and the roadshows were all based smack bang in the middle of the city centres. 'Would you go along to the roadshow and just talk to people there as you're a great example of someone that's changed from person A to person B?' That sounded easy enough.

The roadshows were spread throughout the month of September - the plan was for me to travel by train to each roadshow, stay overnight in a hotel and to either travel home or to the next roadshow, if there was one, the following day. It seemed like an awful lot of effort to go to just to go and talk to people. So it dawned on me - it could be another road trip! So I said, 'Well, maybe I could just connect all these places up with a 28-mile ultra-marathon every day?'

It was time to hit the road again! Road trips are where I feel the happiest - perhaps I could embark on another 'Rory Pilgrimage'? When I suggested it to them, the guys at the agency obviously raised their eyebrows and said, 'Really?'

'Sure! I can do 28 miles a day for 28 days. I have no quibbles about doing that.' So they pitched the idea to Public Health England who loved it. Better still, it was a national campaign which opened up opportunities for me personally to promote myself and my business. They were dead keen! So once the trip was becoming a reality I let them know I would need somebody to look after me - I needed another Sara/Sean like I had on the trip to Lisbon. I suggested my wife Jenny and they agreed which was great. I mean, I wasn't reinventing the wheel here although I think I was sort of reliving Euro 2004 ten years prior. They hired the motorhome, supplied all the food and basically covered all of our expenses - so Jenny and I went on a four-week holiday around the UK!

Don't get me wrong, we worked hard - we did a 28-miler in Sunderland one day and then did one the next day in Bristol which was a heck of a long drive between the two places overnight. Ironically we kicked off the 28-miler in Bristol at the Little Stoke parkrun where Jenny somehow ran a PB. Nonetheless, there were only 15 dates set in stone for the roadshows. I therefore had free reign to choose where I ran for the other 13 days. I chose places that meant a lot to me - the UK was my oyster and I just thought, 'Where shall I go?'

It was a bit like standing in a chocolate shop! First choice: Stratford-upon-Avon, my old hunting ground. I contacted Broad Street Primary - my old infant school - and was invited to go along and take the morning assembly. It was great - I spoke to them all from little four and five year olds up to eleven year olds in the school hall where I'd taken my 11+ (as an adult it seemed a whole lot smaller!)... I was also given a school tour by the school secretary who, funnily enough, I could remember being a baby in her mother's arms. And here she was! She was in her mid-forties and I hadn't seen her for the whole of her life... it was really moving.

Running around Stratford-upon-Avon I met people in the street that I'd known since I was a child. I saw where my father was born and I actually went back to the house where I was born. I went back to my grandparents' old farm in a village called Wolverton and knocked at their old front door. Before I knew it I was talking to the current house-owners, telling them where the well had been when I was a child. They didn't know about it because the house had been completely renovated since then and the well had been covered over. I relived the seventies that day.

In my early running days, I was always appearing in the local press - 'The Stratford-upon-Avon Herald'. I went to school with the editor so I decided to visit their offices as part of my trip down memory lane. I was amazed to see that the same people were still there, 20 years later! It was great to see them again. We were all older but it was like meeting your long lost friends.

I've said it thousands of times but it's time that's the killer - you can't explain it to somebody until they're a bit older, until they're past that big hurdle of 50 when there are likely to be more yesterdays than tomorrows. In terms of big Stoptober moments, it was Day 25 that had a real impact on me. Up until then during the trip I'd listened to the same music over and over again every day. I listened to Rush and to Genesis and I'd just bought the whole Yes back catalogue. I'd gotten into a trance where I'd listen to it all day and it became part of my running rhythm. The marathons were taking between five and six hours so there was no rush at all. It was a simple routine:

I got up and Jenny made me breakfast.

I ran 7 miles.

Mid-morning snack.

I ran 7 miles.

Lunch.

I ran 7 miles.

Afternoon tea.

I ran 7 miles.

Finish, relax, dinner and bed.

Jenny drove the route in the motorhome each day, pulling in at suitable laybys for each of the food breaks to prepare my food and await my arrival.

My heart rate on lots of those runs was under 100bpm, partly due to my fitness and partly due to the slower than usual pace at which I was covering the runs each day. This was necessary to ensure my body remained fresh for the duration of the challenge. My body is very well accustomed to running at this heart rate from all the extreme distances I have run over the years. I run with a lot of people, many of whom are far younger than me but have heart rates of 150bpm plus when we run together. Mine is exceptionally low - resting, it's reached 37bpm.

Running 28 miles a day at a very slow pace, day after day, makes you incredibly fit. But on Day 25 - I'm not kidding - my whole world became clear. Suddenly I had this warm moment of clarity. I'd been wearing one pair of shoes for days which were just perfect. To avoid shin problems, I'd rolled the tongues down and tied them up underneath the laces - it prevents you from getting something called 'anterior compartment syndrome' and is a trick I swear by on mega-day runs. As a bonus it was a great

October - the weather was absolutely glorious. I was running along with no aches and pains, I had no fatigue, nothing at all like that, and it felt like my feet weren't even touching the floor. It was one of those out-of-body experiences - at that moment I reached Rory-Euphoria!

I suppose it was my serotonin and endorphin levels being completely overloaded from being on the road for so many days! My whole rhythm - my whole body rhythm, my whole life rhythm, everything - was in place. The sun was shining. It was just a real life moment. It was perfect. I just thought, 'This is it.' It was a bit like that moment I experienced on the way to Lisbon. If you could bottle it, you'd be a millionaire. Ironically, it happened on the A4 on the way into Swindon. Now Swindon is not exactly the most romantic of places, so it's funny to imagine everything in my mind suddenly slotting into place there. Most people are happy to be leaving Swindon but I was in Rory-Euphoria entering it! All of my body's biorhythms felt right; my heart rate averaged 100bpm that day.

My mid-morning snack had routinely become strawberry milkshake followed by fried egg and bacon sandwiches drenched in tomato sauce. Jenny had perfected them by then. Why my obsession with these sandwiches? Because of the high sugar content that I needed to keep me moving. In fact, as an aside, as part of the challenge we actually agreed to provide data for a study being undertaken by Kingston University from our 28 days on the road. Jenny meticulously logged every single thing I consumed each day taking photos of every single meal, box, carton and packet. When you're not running, your body can usually process about 60g of carbohydrate per hour - they calculated that I was processing a massive 103g of carbohydrate per hour. I'd become a Carbo-Blast-Furnace because of the amount of energy I was expending each day.

Don't get me wrong - I lost a good stone doing this run even though I was taking on lots and lots of high calorie foods. To make up for the calorie shortfall though, I was literally burning my own body fat as fuel for 28 days. And when I wasn't on the road I was blogging, Facebooking and attending TV and press interviews to promote the campaign - that's the way that it worked. I started running in the middle of September as the pre-event media story. I was scheduled to run 28 miles a day for 21 days, arrive in Trafalgar Square for the big press launch of the Stoptober campaign on 1st October and then complete the remaining 7 days running home to Cardiff.

So the idea was to run into Trafalgar Square all triumphant, and then run 150 miles home to Cardiff because the Welsh Government had recently embraced the campaign for Wales. It just so happened that the Cardiff Half Marathon fell on the 28th day. I decided to run 15 miles in the morning before the Cardiff Half Marathon meaning I could do that race as the grand finale.

Better still, the press couldn't believe I was going to run home from London. It was great, especially running into Wales over the Old Severn Bridge which is very dear to my heart as I was there when it opened in 1966. There's something magical about that bridge for me - we went there on a day out when I was very, very young and, running over it and back into Wales was just an amazing thing to do nearly half a century after my childhood visit.

It's funny looking back on Stoptober. We had this big mobile home - I'm not kidding, it was HUGE - and Jenny drove it all the way around the UK. We clocked up over 3,000 miles in this seven-berth home-from-home. We thought it would be a good idea to join the Caravan Club so we could stay at one of their sites each night. We turned out to be the worst behaved Caravan Club members ever. Very quickly it became glaringly apparent that most Caravan Club members were of an older generation with very different ideals. Firstly, the average arrival time seemed to be around 11:00am with many campers taking a mid-afternoon siesta around 3:00pm. This was a far cry from our

6:00-10:00pm arrival when the sites were typically locked up for the night. Sometimes we would see the site wardens who were usually wondering where we had got to and, more often than not, had marked us down as a 'no show'. We would then either grudgingly be allowed to drive to our pitch waking everyone up in the process with our noisy engine and headlights, or be offered a 'latecomers' bay external to the site. Within a week we were blacklisted. We kept receiving angry emails stating that we weren't abiding by club rule X sub-section Y, point 1 and eventually we weren't allowed to stay on their sites anymore. It took a grovelling telephone call to them, explaining our predicament and asking if we could retain our membership for a further three weeks, after which we promised we would never book onto a site ever again! Luckily they understood and actually they were very accommodating thereon in.

28 days is quite a long time and after a few days we got into a routine: you get up in the morning, you prepare the motorhome to move - lock everything down, unplug the electric, unplug the water - and then you drive to the start of that day's 28-mile journey. Plus, we needed to fit in press every morning and often throughout the day. Our press events on 15 of the days involved blowing up a huge red inflatable ball with STOP printed on it in big white letters. This was then rolled through busy town centres for about an hour and a half before reaching the respective roadshow and mingling with the public before heading off by ourselves to either finish the run or drive to the next campsite.

There were some days where I thought, 'Gosh, it's going to be a really big press call today - I'd better run the 28 miles before we start.' On those days we had a mega-early start. Sometimes we would complete half of the run before the press call and then finish it off afterwards - that was the job, just like London to Lisbon, for four weeks.

So how exhausting was the running? Actually, do you know what? It wasn't. I was doing the thing I love and I was the centre of attention. I couldn't get it much better than that, could I? Oh, and I was being paid to do it! Even better!

It was another one of those rare opportunities, like London to Lisbon, where I had the time to think everything through in my head, whilst living, enjoying the now. It was another break from the trials and tribulations of everyday life. You park them up, don't you? That's why the MdS is so good for me - you park up life for 11 days and go and live in the desert. Nobody can email you about work when you're out there. During this '28-in-28' challenge I couldn't see clients to give them personal training sessions or fitness tests or write them plans - I was on the road.

Furthermore, in contrast to London to Lisbon, I enjoyed the additional benefit of publicity - the Government continuously sent out Tweets about me for the duration of the challenge. My audience, therefore, was suddenly a whole lot bigger. I also revisited some of the grounds I'd visited during my football ground tour back in 2002 including Manchester United and Sunderland AFC. More trips down memory lane.

Plus, it was interesting in some ways to have Jenny as my morale-boosting coach. You have to have support - you can't do everything by yourself no matter how much of a macho man you feel you are. We had our moments. There's a thing called the Brunel Mood Scale which I was asked to fill in first thing in the morning and last thing at night every day as part of the Kingston University study. It's a chart comprising 20 emotions and you score yourself from 'Not Very' to 'Extremely' for each of them. So there might be 'Happy', 'Sad'... 'Bitter' was one of them - I remember that one especially! It's funny as I'd never consider myself as bitter, ever, because I don't feel that I'm a bitter person. But there was one day when Jenny got lost buying me a cake. She was getting the cake as a surprise for my 800th marathon but she'd got lost finding her way back to the day's running route. I'd got to the end of the run - it was on a long, straight road out of Bristol down the A4, and I couldn't believe how anyone could get lost on that.

But actually she was trying to buy this bloody cake. So at the end of that day, I was most definitely 'Extremely' in the 'Bitter' column! It was interesting to analyse the mood trends after the challenge. It basically showed that, in the morning before a run, your moods are fairly tempered - you're not strongly agreeing or disagreeing with stuff. You're 'Fairly' - 'Well, I'm fairly happy, yeah. Am I sad? Fairly sad I suppose,' or whatever. Are you feeling Fairly energetic? 'Yeah, okay.' Tired? 'Fairly tired, not very tired.'

But by the end of the day, you're 'Extremely'. Are you happy? 'I'm Extremely happy.' Are you fatigued? 'Not fatigued at all.' Are you tired? 'No, not at all.' My whole mood was different after the run. It was fascinating to see how the running had perhaps triggered certain chemical reactions in my brain and affected my general sense of wellbeing.

The charts had been around at the Flora 1,000 Mile Challenge in 2003. At the time I thought they were quite negative and didn't want them to dampen my mood given I was effectively running a very drawn out race. This time though, given there was no racing element to the challenge, I thought it would be really interesting to do. It also gave the guys at Kingston University a really good insight into the sorts of emotions and stresses I experienced over the 28 days.

We're all different, aren't we? Some things matter more than others to each of us. Whenever I meet a new client, I always ask them about the condition of the inside of their car. If it's super-clean and super-neat, it means that they really care about their environment, for instance, and about what people think of them. On the other hand, if it's an absolute farmyard in there, maybe that's what they're like as a person.

It's about standards, isn't it? My standards are: when I coach people, I always wear my smart coaching, running gear.

It always matches and it always looks really presentable. I'm always clean-shaven and look the part because that's how I want to be seen - that I'm being professional. That's something else I have in common with Peter Gabriel! My God! The bloke looked brilliant and he's a pensioner. He looked absolutely fantastic! I know he's a multi-millionaire, but he's really professional about how he looks - his whole brand. I think it's really important how you portray yourself, so if a client's car is erring more on the side of a farmyard, I tell them, 'Well, go and tidy it up!'

I don't want to be the unattractive fat person with a beard, drinking and smoking, because in days gone by I've also been at that end of the spectrum. I hate it. The motorhome we lived in for Stoptober was always neat and orderly. There really was a place for everything and everything was in its place. It had to be, because with the amount of gear we needed for the challenge the space was very limited, even on a seven-berth motorhome. Often we were carrying the inflatable STOP ball and we had Rocky the dog on board too. There had to be a method to doing things - an order to it.

I didn't drive it, I didn't have to - Jenny drove it. Imagine your wife reversing a 4.3-metre-long giant motorhome, reversing it into a tight parking space. As a guy, we sort of put our hands over our eyes, don't we? Or we say, 'Excuse me, love - I'll do it for you.' I didn't do any of that. She did all of it, because she was in charge of that part of the run. Everybody had key roles and responsibilities. It was military precision. I didn't have to worry about anything. I didn't have to worry about her being in a certain place at a certain time, apart from when she was buying the bloody cake, because I knew she'd be there. I had absolute faith and commitment that she would be there for me.

So there was only that one day when I was 'Bitter'. In the mornings I did feel tired - how could you not running 28 miles a day without a break for 28 days? Some mornings I actually felt very indifferent about doing the run at all. If you're 13 days in and you've got 15 left to go, you think, 'Well, okay, I'm nearly halfway. That's all right.' The first thing I always checked out was the weather - was it raining? Have I mentioned that I hate running in the rain?! Luckily, it didn't rain very much and the weather was pretty good. Nonetheless, given it was September and we were in the UK there were inevitably some days when it tipped down. That's when I pontificated - I put it off thinking, 'Oh well, I'll just put it off a bit - I'll have a tinker with my shoes and I'll have a tinker with whatever.' In my experience most runners exhibit this personality trait. I certainly did when it was raining - particularly if there was no roadshow that day and all I had to do was complete 28 miles as the pressure was off. On the days where you had to run into a city centre and attend a press launch it was very different. You had to be at a certain place at a certain time and you couldn't be late. On those days I had to plan my route meticulously. At the outset, the PR agency tried to plan routes for me but this didn't work so in the end I just said, 'Thanks very much but don't worry about wasting your time planning the routes - I'll do my own.'

Of course I preferred it because it meant I was in control. 'I'll run wherever I want to thanks very much... fair enough if I need to be at certain places at certain times, but for the rest of the time don't tell me where to run - I'll sort it out!' This also added a lot to the freedom of the adventure. I loaded my routes onto my computer every day for accountability - to prove to people that I'd done it. You certainly don't want onlookers to say, 'Well you didn't do it.' And have nothing to prove them wrong. I made sure that they were exactly 28 miles, to the step.

To be certain I'd normally say to Jenny, 'Meet me at 27 miles, so I know where 27 miles is, and then I can run half-a-mile and then come back, Captain Barclay style.' Total Distance OCD. I ran all over the UK. I ran on the Wirral, Liverpool, Manchester and Hexham on the north-east coast. I went to places I'd never even heard of. I did a couple in Thatcham, Berkshire, because that's where my sister lives. We parked the motorhome outside her house, ate some proper food and had a bath. It felt amazing to be properly clean.

We also went to my parents' house in Doncaster as one of the runs was up in Leeds. We spent three days at Stratford Racecourse - I even went to the first place that I ever started running - Sidelands Road in Stratford-upon-Avon. There was the very pavement where I took my first running step. It was such a good feeling to go back.

The beauty of the Stoptober challenge was that the Government had partnered with the Army who were helping to roll this giant red ball into some of the town centres. On Day 21 the plan was for a big group of us to run into Trafalgar Square. It was like the 'triumphant finish' to my past 20 years of running. I can remember going there as a young boy of seven - we went on a trip to London on the train and I'd been so excited about climbing on the lions. Here I was 40-odd years later, running in, feeling like I was seven years old again but also being followed by all these soldiers, and being greeted in the middle of the square by Dame Sally Davis and Professor Kevin Fenton from Public Health England. A number of friends and celebrities had come along to see me too and I felt very important!

Maybe that's what it is. Maybe that's what I want at the end of the day. I want to feel important and to make my mark. For me, Day 21 was a triumphant climax to a 20-year span of being free from alcohol and cigarettes and pioneering mega-day distance running - it felt like a reward for my 'services to running'... like I was there receiving my own Running OBE. The interesting thing was that it had more meaning to me than almost all of my other running challenges because I was the only person doing it.

Stoptober had that real 'Wow' factor - I ran 196 miles a week for four weeks, a total of 784 miles - that's a long way! I often found that when I was explaining the event to people, the standard response would be, 'So where's the rest of the team running it?' Many a jaw dropped when I let them know that, actually, there wasn't anyone else running apart from me.

The final day - the 28th marathon in Cardiff - that was hilarious. I planned to finish with the Cardiff Half Marathon, which is 13.1 miles for the less running-obsessed reader. So I had to get up at four o'clock in the morning because I had to run 14.9 miles before the race. I thought, 'Well, I'm always running in Cardiff - where shall I go?' I decided to go down and have a look at the stands and the finish line of the race.

Both the start and finish of the race were down in the centre of the city, so you can imagine what it looked like at 4:30am... it was like Vietnam! People literally littered the streets - there were beer tins and fish and chip wrappers everywhere; people were fighting outside Burger King. I ran through the middle of Cardiff looking at this world that I would have been a part of 20 years previously feeling, I suppose, very self-righteous. It's quite astonishing how quickly it all got cleaned up - at around 6:00am the whole of the city seemed to be spring cleaned by this team of people. They eradicated all of the leftovers from the night before and, cher-ching, Cardiff was then ready for the race.

I came home, ate some breakfast and went down to the race start with Jenny. From then onwards I became one of the 14,000 strong field of runners and ran a 1:49 which I was really pleased with. During the race, I ran alongside people running that sort of distance for the first time ever, just like I had back in 1994 at Stratford-upon-Avon. They were so overjoyed just to get to the finish line in their first ever race. Then here I was, having already completed my first half-marathon of the day and feeling uber-fit after finishing 28 x 28-milers in 28 days.

It was another one of those 'jigsaw moments' where everything just slotted into place. I got to the finish line and felt totally overwhelmed. Jenny was battling the marshals to make sure she got a great finisher's photo of me and the Stoptober photographer took a fantastic photo of me popping a bottle of champagne, of all things.

It was a bitter-sweet feeling as I was also a little sad that the 28 marathons were over. I now felt a little crestfallen as running an ultra-marathon every day had become second nature and I would have loved to carry on. This pilgrimage, however, was now over. Funnily enough, the next day I went for a 10 mile run - my body had become so accustomed to running distance every day that I had to detune for quite a few days afterwards. About three weeks later, I ran my quickest marathon for 11 years at Abingdon. After 28 marathons I felt really slim, fit and positive about myself and about life - I smashed it!

I'm somebody that needs the outdoors and daily exercise - a bit like a dog. I might be in my fifties, but actually I'm more like an eight-year-old boisterous child that you have to take down to the park to wear out. When I was a very young child at Broad Street Primary, Mrs Davis - one of the dinner ladies - used to encourage me to run laps of the school playground. She would time each lap and as I finished it she'd say, 'Right, go and run another one.'

After the Abingdon Marathon I went into hibernation, from racing at least, waking up for Mick McGeoch's Barry 40 in March 2014. From December 2013 until early March 2014 this was the focus of all my training. I spent three months clocking up more miles and building up to give myself the best possible opportunity of running 40 miles - that's 161 laps around a track - in six hours. Yes, I was running the MdS three weeks later but I wasn't bothered about achieving a good time/position there that year - it was all about the Barry 40. I had a really good race - I felt really energised from all the training and boosted by the prog rock on my mp3 player. I just zoned out for the whole race and ran it hard all the way.

I think those 28 days on the road helped me to strip myself

down and re-emerge as a new-improved self. It was a bit like a ten year pruning where I dropped all the baggage I'd built up over that time - emotional baggage, home baggage, life baggage. When you're out on the road you don't need very much so it makes you more aware of what's important and what isn't important. I got to learn so much about myself. Plus, the running was great because it taught me deep down that I really, really love bacon and egg sandwiches.

Stoptober was also about all of the people that we met. We didn't meet a single person that was anything other than nice, kind and enthusiastic about what we were doing. I spoke to so many people who smoked - all of them wanted to give up. It was really quite nice to give them a personal message and say, 'Well, I don't expect you to go and run 1,000 marathons or set world records, but maybe life will be a whole lot better if you give up. You never know. There might be a lot of life out there that you're not aware of.'

Am I going to stop when I get to 1,000? People are quick to hand out their advice, 'Well, you'll slow down when you get to 1,000 marathons won't you?' I'm thinking, 'Like hell I will.'

Life - it will end in a number, won't it? How old are you going to be when you finally kick the bucket?! Will you be 64, 73 - I don't know - 91, 103? We don't know what that last number is, do we? It's going to be like that with my marathons. I mean, will it be 1,071, 1,523, or is it going to stay at today's 976? I don't know. In actual fact I don't want to know because I'm quite happy doing what I'm doing right now, and I'd love to be able to do it for the rest of my life.

It's the uncertainty - that's what can make us feel out of control. I do like to feel in control but I also like life to be a little bit spontaneous. Is there another 'Big Running Challenge' out there? I hope there is as I'm a surfer who hasn't yet surfed his biggest wave...

# CHAPTER ELEVEN

## TIME FOR CHANGE

### AND I WILL KISS - UNDERWORLD 2012

*During the opening ceremony of the 2012 London Olympics there was a moment that I'll never forget. To be honest, I had pretty low expectations and was looking at Danny Boyle's £9m creation in mild disbelief at the beginning of the show. Then, over the course of a few minutes, it transformed into a jaw-dropping spectacle that made every hair on my body stand on end. The 17:15 minute track was written by Underworld's Rick Smith and features 1,200 musicians including Dame Evelyn Glennie on percussion and The Pandemonium Drummers. The ceremony's grand finale featured Sir Kenneth Branagh as Sir Isambard Kingdom Brunel and there was a breathtaking moment where all five blazing rings were hoisted into place to finally pour molten sparks to the ground. The title makes reference to a speech given by Caliban in Act 2, Scene 2 of The Tempest by William Shakespeare which seems so apt given my Stratford-upon-Avon connection. I have run some of my fastest times listening to this track as it's so inspiring.*

Before setting off to the MdS 2015 with Sir Ranulph Fiennes, we were both invited to appear on BBC Breakfast with presenters Charlie Stayt and Naga Munchetty. I've always wanted to be on BBC Breakfast so it was brilliant to finally sit on the Sofa!

Actually, it was both brilliant and scary as I was praying that I didn't make a complete idiot of myself.

I think the media training course that I attended back in 2003 for the Flora 1,000 Mile Challenge stood me in good stead - we were taught what to say and what not to say on TV. My message was simple - total support for Sir Ranulph because it was his gig. The charity, Marie Curie, had got us both the slot but we were there because of him. So when asked, 'What's it like training with Sir Ranulph?' I said, 'Well, it's like running across the desert carrying a Ming vase, a priceless Ming vase.' Funnily enough, that was a sound-bite they then tweeted out. It's true though - he's a national institution. He's 72 years old and he's accomplished so many incredible adventures.

The media is a great vehicle for me and I've appeared on BBC Breakfast before, but never in the studio. You can try really hard to get there by yourself doing your own stunts but sometimes you have to piggy back on a bigger name, which is just what I did with Sir Ranulph. Training him has given me so much kudos as a coach. So when the world's greatest living explorer 'phones you up and says, 'Can you train me?' it's like someone asking a musician, 'Do you want to come and play with Pink Floyd?'

We followed the TV interview with thirteen back to back radio interviews. January is always a good time for a fitness story - New Year's resolutions coupled with the fact that there's not a lot else going on in the news. In the long, dark depressing days of winter people need a ray of sunshine; they enjoy hearing about real life heroes like Sir Ranulph because he's just one in a billion and someone to look up to and aspire to.

A lot of people are following me these days which has both its advantages and drawbacks. Obviously I enjoy being in the public eye and all that comes with it. From a personal perspective, however, at every race I run these days there seem to be people looking over their shoulders whilst running along to make sure they are beating me. There's no option to compete under the radar anymore which I must say would make a refreshing change sometimes.

I've spent 22 years being different to most people. Most people go to work, play hard, have time to themselves, go to the pub and they're quite happy with their lot. I don't do that sort of stuff - I run. Nonetheless, as the world of ultra-running becomes increasingly popular, I'm finding that more and more people want to do what I'm doing. The analogy I often use is that, for years, I have been on my own basking in the sunshine on my little ultra-running desert island, but now it's all getting a bit crowded. I'm not quite sure if I'm all that happy about being joined by the crowds! It feels like they're all jumping on my bandwagon.

And actually, I'm not quite sure whether all the people joining me on my desert island are treating this fantastic thing that I've found with the respect that it really deserves. Maybe they're seeing it as a bit of a stepping stone to a new job or a new life. Maybe it's a station in their life journey and they just don't see it with the 'Rory Euphoria' vision that I do. I'd like many of them to leave my island but that's not going to happen. I have to accept that, in accomplishing all of my running challenges and living the dream both from a running and a publicity perspective, it was inevitable that onlookers would want to join the party!

On the plus side, it's actually these people that make my coaching career possible. At the end of the day, running has been a conduit to a different place with different horizons. For me, it's really obvious how you get the most out of this running lark... plainly obvious in fact. It isn't, so it seems, for most and I really enjoy offering them my help and guidance to reach their running potential.

When I was in the print game, the original apprenticeship was six years long - it became worthless when it was reduced to a two-year apprenticeship, then they stopped it altogether. Nowadays, people avoid going to the school of hard knocks to do the prerequisite suffering - they skip the hard work by simply buying the relevant knowledge. That also applies to running...

I've found out the hard way - I've spent 22 years learning my trade. Perhaps I shouldn't have been so solitary in the early stages of my running career. It took me ages to let anybody know what I was up to because I was cleaning myself up. I was frightened that I might not be able to stick to my new lifestyle - that I would ruin all my hard work and revert to the person I was before. I was running away from the horrible Rory Coleman that I used to be - the out-of-control person that really didn't know anything. I'd picked up really bad behavioural characteristics that were basically destroying me.

I feel both proud and extremely lucky that I managed to pull myself out of a nosedive before I hit the ground and crashed out of this life. I also believe I have helped to make my own luck... I'm a very positive person. I blog every day - I try not to blog anything negative - my glass is always full.

So yes, it's been a solitary existence, but it's also been a really happy one. I've really enjoyed finding out what works and what doesn't work for me - the right shoes, the right socks. I've found out how to get up and run day after day after day after day. I've worked it out. I'm really proud of that. It's taken me years - a lifetime in fact. It goes back to this ageing rock star thing doesn't it? You don't acquire star quality overnight when you are pioneering something new. These days, however, my clients can shortcut all that experience and experimentation by paying for my time and my knowledge. It's bitter-sweet I suppose but it pays the bills so I can't be too disgruntled about it!

I was ecstatic appearing on BBC Breakfast, I was ecstatic running to Lisbon and running around the Premier League football grounds. I can remember 2 April, 1995 - I don't know what you were doing on that date? You probably can't even remember one day in 1995. I can as it was my first London Marathon. When I recollect all those experiences I feel really happy and really proud of myself because I've discovered the wonder of running myself rather than having it handed to me.

I've met a million runners and I talk to hundreds of people every week about running. I find it really easy to see what they're all about because I've learnt so much about what makes people tick, especially in the last eight years or so since I've embraced coaching as my chosen career. Sometimes I can see my own traits in clients that I train, on other occasions I can see traits that I have long discarded in favour of a fitter and healthier lifestyle. It can be a bit like looking at a reflection of my former self. When you run with clients for five hours you really share a lot with each other - it's often a very therapeutic way for them to exorcise their demons and a great opportunity for me to prune bits off them too. To do this I have to trawl back through the parts of myself I don't want to - but it helps me to be a much more effective life coach.

I feel healed - I am a good teacher because I've sorted my own shit out - I guess that sort of makes me a healer too. I certainly know that I've helped a lot of clients emerge from some pretty dark and depressing periods in their lives intact which gives me a great deal of pleasure and fulfilment.

Given so much of my running is spent in the company of clients, I must say I do love it when I go running on my own with my prog rock in hand - that's what I love doing. Funnily enough, I believe I can live without running but I can't live without music.

I keep my work routes and my own training routes separate to keep it all fresh. That's important to me as is that wonderful calm feeling you get post-run when you've started out feeling angry, upset or confused. Sometimes, life can become this sort of giant clouded fish tank which you can end up drowning in - all the water is just swirling around and all the mud from the bottom is clouding the way. Running cleanses and filters all that cloudy water - you go for a run and by the time you get back, lots of those things have then been processed and put into their right place. So in that respect, running has given me a certain amount of clarity in my life. In fact there have been moments when I've just been totally euphoric and suddenly seen things, people and situations for what they really are.

I'm not a sheep. Pink Floyd's 'Sheep' is a really important anthem to me. I don't want to be out there on the pasture just harmlessly passing my time away. Roger Waters summed up life perfectly for me with that song. Do you want to pass away your time?

I recently ran a client to Barry Island and along the seafront outside Gavin & Stacey's chip shop. The rain was horizontal. I'm not kidding - it really was horizontal. If I'd jumped into the sea I couldn't have been any wetter. You know how much I hate the rain by now but do you know what, it was such an easy day of running. The client was great anyway - he's always good fun - and I just thought, 'I'm going to bask in the rain here and enjoy the ride as I could be sat in an office.' I bet no-one else was doing what I did with my work life that day. That's what it feels like to be solitary on your island.

Soon I will have been running for more than half of my adult lifetime which feels great. My world and the real world have changed a lot since 1994. Back then we were pre-Internet and everybody wore double-breasted suits - fashion was very different. The Spice Girls hadn't been invented, Pink Floyd played in trendy white t-shirts and Genesis were rubbish.

Take cars for example. Back in 1994, everybody in the print game had a Sierra or a Cavalier with a mandatory go faster fin on the boot. These days, people drive cars that have the lowest $CO_2$ emissions with maximum energy efficiency and minimal running costs. We've changed. If you look at footballers back in 1993 when the Premier League started they were all very lean and wore tiny porn shorts! Players are a lot chunkier now; in fact the whole population has grown. Smoking is now outlawed in public places. How on earth was it ever legal to smoke in pubs and clubs?! I remember having to step outside of some of my regular haunts to take some fresh air because my eyes were watering so much from the smoke. Your clothes smelt like you'd been standing next to a bonfire after a night out.

Twenty-two years on we have Google and Facebook to fill our lives. We're different. I'm different. Everyone's different. Life's not a bed of roses nowadays, is it? It's not all white fluffy bunnies and blue skies and green fields. Life's hard. Life's a lot harder now than it was in 1994. People are busier. There's a lot more pressure. Everybody feels it. How pressured do you feel right now? You feel compelled to do things. People expect you to go out and get drunk with them or to go to parties. There's a lot of peer pressure to do things that you might not necessarily want to do.

It feels like I'm closing my book on an era here, on my last 22 years. Why? I need to ring-fence all of my achievements up until now. I believe a new chapter of my life is beginning. I believe it's time to go and broaden my horizons. Maybe I need to go back to basics.

Sir Ranulph is in his seventies and he's in really good shape for his age but I wonder how many more adventures he will have completed by the time he reaches 80. My parents are in their eighties and they certainly won't be crossing any polar ice-caps any time soon. Sir Ranulph is only 18 years older than me, so I'm beginning to feel this sense of urgency to fit in as much as I possibly can before my age gets the better of me. The battle with Old Father Time is at the forefront of my thoughts right now.

Thankfully, age doesn't affect my business - quite the contrary in fact. The more extraordinary feats you do, the more clients like to meet you because you've done what they want to do. They are desperate for inspiration, nurturing and knowledge to help them shortcut as much as they can.

At the time of writing I feel a strong urge to leave my now crowded desert island and find another deserted one. I'm not the same person I was when I embarked on my running journey. My tastes have changed over those years and so have my needs. On average I've run six miles a day for the last 8,000 days and my love affair with running hasn't dwindled. I still get the same kick from running today that I did when I first started. That's an awesome feeling. On a recent trip to the post office I forgot my wallet - what a twit - so I jogged home, picked it up and jogged back. You don't see many people jogging around our area but I do, because that's what I do.

I admit that my running has had a detrimental effect on my family, on my marriages and on the amount of time I've spent with my children. It has had a detrimental effect on all of the people that I've lived with. It comes at a cost and I've had to consider whether it's all been worthwhile whilst writing this book. I've had to offset that cost against making it to 54 years of age and being a much better person.

Life's a riddle - if I knew all the answers I'd be a millionaire. Clearly I don't and I'm just working my way through it as best I can. I'm quite happy with how I've got to where I am today - the road certainly hasn't been straight but it has been an exciting journey with lots of really positive experiences along the way. I've had the opportunity to do so many amazing things and meet so many fantastic people. I think I've met more interesting people than I would have met if I hadn't run and I've been to, well, some unbelievable places on the planet. I've also gotten inside buildings and TV studios that most people never get to see. I'm confident there are plenty more amazing experiences left for me to enjoy - at least that's what I'm pinning my hopes on.

I'm in it for the long haul. I compare a lot of the people I coach to contestants on 'The X Factor' - they'll be great for a couple of singles, maybe an album, and then they'll fade away and do something else. On the other hand I'm more like Peter Gabriel, not a flash in the pan but a lifelong stalwart and pioneer of ultra-running.

Without running my life would have been very different, maybe I wouldn't still be here. Running is therapy to me. I've got the Pearl. I really have got it. I've found my utopia. I know what's made me tick - I just want to hold onto it. It's got a lovely radioactive glow to it, I want to feel the warmth from it because I know one day sadly it will burn out.

Right now I'm going somewhere different - on a new mission perhaps... I can feel it in my bones. Right now I feel like I'm in a transition phase. When am I going to stop counting all those years that I've been running? I've got to the end of the birthday cards in the local shop - you can get a 21$^{st}$ birthday card - the next one's 30. I can't get myself a 'Happy 23$^{rd}$ Birthday' card because Clintons don't sell them. I need to move on from my well-worn story... 'Well, you know, it's 22 years ago since I was an idiot.' That's been my story for a long time now so it's all becoming a bit passé. I talk about there being fewer tomorrows than yesterdays. Maybe I'm also going into the next phase frightened. But that's ok as I have 22 years of confidence to rely on.

I still want to pioneer new adventures and challenges. I want to be the guy that everyone remembers in the future, I want to be the guy that everyone says, 'You were one of the pioneers, you did it first.'

Maybe Paula Radcliffe has the same lingering questions in her mind - maybe she's having the same conversations with herself right now. I think it's harder for her because she ran 2 hours, 15 minutes and 25 seconds at The London Marathon in 2003, and it's been downhill for her ever since. She can't run any races now as people are always looking at her times. The fun of racing has gone for her.

Paula's surfed her biggest wave. I'm still enjoying mine as whatever it is that I'm doing now with my running feels elastic. I'm running on treadmills, I'm running back-to-back ultras… all whilst teaching other people how to do it and clocking up even more marathons. I go to bed happy in the knowledge that I'm sticking out and that life's still an adventure for me.

As far as the MdS is concerned, I know I have to perform whenever I go - you can't teach folk how to do the race if you're a backmarker, or worse still if you drop out. Gosh that would affect my mortgage! If you're going to be an authority on something you've got to walk the walk and talk the talk. That's what I plan to do - to carry on building up my expertise and credibility as a coach.

In 1999 I ran 86 marathons, I set five Guinness World Records in a day, I ran in marathons across the world and I raced across Jordan. By December that year I couldn't get out of bed. I was completely destroyed. Three weeks after the '28-in-28' I ran my best marathon time in 11 years. After that I took a well-earned rest as I didn't want the 1999 burn out again. I've learnt so much about myself - what makes me tick, when to stop.

I see it now with the people that I coach. They've got momentum from seeing me and they do really well for a few weeks. Then they just lose their way, only to find it again when they come back and see me. They get complacent and take their foot off the gas. Absolute concentration is what's needed and I think that's why I've been successful.

You've got to work, you've got to get up, you've got to go shopping, you've got to do all your household stuff, you've got to be nice to your partner - you've got to do all those things and, by the way, you've got to run a load of miles as the more you run the better you get.

It's so easy to procrastinate but in your heart of hearts you have to think, 'Just pull your finger out and do the session you should be doing.' When you've done it you'll be as happy as Larry. Yes, it takes valuable time, but that's time well spent - not wasted in the pub. I've certainly found it a very positive thing to do. It isn't complicated - you step outside your front door and you run. You run for as long as you like and then you come back. It's really simple, or at least you'd think so...

Running is actually a very psychological sport - it isn't really about your legs. You may be running across deserts overlooking mind-blowing vistas, meeting amazing people, experiencing highs and lows as you struggle up summits, defining yourself as you push yourself harder than you've ever imagined... and you may be standing out from the crowd, not being a sheep, becoming one of The Greats... but as Britain's Most Extreme Runner, I've learnt over the past two decades that the real majesty of long-distance running takes place in your mind.